Brief Coaching

G000310746

Brief Coaching: A Solution Focused Approach offers a new approach to coaching by considering how the client will know when they have reached their goal, and what they are already doing to get there. The coach aims to work towards the solution rather than working away from the problem, so that the client's problem is not central to the session, but instead the coach and the client work towards the client's preferred future.

This book employs case examples and transcripts of sessions to offer guidance on:

- looking for resources rather than deficits
- exploring possible and preferred futures
- examining what is already contributing to that future
- treating clients as experts in all aspects of their lives.

This practical guide includes summaries and activities for the coach to do with the client and will therefore be a useful tool for both new and experienced coaches, as well as therapists branching into coaching who want to add to their existing skills.

Chris Iveson, Evan George and **Harvey Ratner** are founding members of BRIEF, an independent training, therapy and consultation agency in the practice of solution focused brief therapy.

Essential Coaching Skills and Knowledge
Series Editors: Gladeana McMahon,
Stephen Palmer & Averil Leimon

The **Essential Coaching Skills and Knowledge** series provides an accessible and lively introduction to key areas in the developing field of coaching. Each title in the series is written by leading coaches with extensive experience and has a strong practical emphasis, including illustrative vignettes, summary boxes, exercises and activities. Assuming no prior knowledge, these books will appeal to professionals in business, management, human resources, psychology, counselling and psychotherapy, as well as students and tutors of coaching and coaching psychology.

www.routledgementalhealth.com/essential-coaching-skills

Titles in the series:

Developmental Coaching: Life Transitions and Generational Perspectives
Edited by Stephen Palmer & Sheila Panchal

Cognitive Behavioural Coaching in Practice: An Evidence Based Approach
Edited by Michael Neenan & Stephen Palmer

Brief Coaching

A Solution Focused Approach

*Chris Iveson, Evan George
and Harvey Ratner*

Routledge
Taylor & Francis Group

LONDON AND NEW YORK

First published 2012
by Routledge
27 Church Road, Hove, East Sussex, BN3 2FA

Simultaneously published in the USA and Canada
by Routledge
711 Third Avenue, New York NY 10017

Routledge is an imprint of the Taylor & Francis Group, an Informa business

British Library Cataloguing-in-Publication Data
A catalogue record for this book is available from the British Library

Library of Congress Cataloging in Publication Data
Iveson, Chris.
Brief coaching: a solution focused approach / Chris Iveson, Evan George
and Harvey Ratner.
      p. cm.
Includes bibliographical references and index.
   ISBN 978–0–415–66746–3 (hbk.) – ISBN 978–0–415–66747–0 (pbk.)
1. Brief psychotherapy. 2. Personal coaching. 3. Counseling psychology.
4. Counseling psychologist and client. I. George, Evan. II. Ratner,
Harvey. III. Title.
   RC480.55.I94 2012
   616.89'147—dc23

                                                    2011026539

                       ISBN: 978–0–415–66746–3 (hbk)
                       ISBN: 978–0–415–66747–0 (pbk)
                       ISBN: 978–0–203–14441–1 (ebk)

                    Typeset in Century Schoolbook MT by
                       RefineCatch Limited, Bungay, Suffolk

                    Printed and bound in Great Britain by
                 TJ International Ltd, Padstow, Cornwall

Contents

Preface

We hope this book will be a practical guide by which both new and experienced coaches can add to their skills. Deceptively simple in its basic principles solution focused conversations are far from easy to conduct. For one thing they are counter-intuitive: they lead us to be curious about what is adjacent to the issue rather than the issue itself; they lead us to look at the apparently insignificant small print of life while largely ignoring the headlines; and they lead us to look back, not from the present, but from the future.

It is almost impossible to appreciate the apparent marginality of a solution focused coaching conversation without actually showing one and to this end the book contains many illustrative portions of transcript. It will often seem as if very little is happening. There are no epiphanous moments, no life-changing insights and little drama beyond the kitchen sink. A coaching client might not even remember much of the conversation. Yet only two or three sessions – and often only one – are likely to have an enormously creative impact.

One of the most common solution focused mantras is 'leave no footprints'. By staying on the edge, keeping out of the client's business and trusting to the solution focused process the coach becomes a witness to successes that may not otherwise have happened and in which he or she appears to have played no visible part. As one client said at the end of three sessions, 'I know I would be dead if I hadn't come to see you but it is important that I say that you have played no part in my life'. The coach was touched and replied, 'Thank you. And you have played no part in mine. But I will always remember you'. 'And I'll always remember you' she said with a smile.

Acknowledgements

We originally taught ourselves solution focus from Steve de Shazer's early books, *Keys* (1985) and *Clues* (1988). These books had been heavily criticised as 'cookbooks' with the implication that therapy neither could nor should be so simply codified, but 25 years on these self same books have been the basis for the solution focused cookery classes, dinner parties and restaurants that can be found all over the world. The solution focused approach is being used and adapted wherever change is needed. de Shazer always, with huge diffidence, claimed that all he did was watch his wife Insoo Kim Berg working with clients and write down what she did and both of them in their different ways continued to influence our work until their deaths. Of the many other colleagues around the world one who has helped and influenced our thinking (and began his solution focused journey even earlier than we did) is Harry Korman in Sweden. Through his management of the international Solution focused therapy email forum (SFT-L) Harry has brought together an immensely creative gathering that has also been a support and a generator of helpful ideas.

We have also been inspired, especially in this venture, by many colleagues from the business world who have so ably shown that a solution focus applies as well to coaching and leadership as it does to therapy. Of these Mark McKergow and Paul Z. Jackson have been both supporters and leaders. Lastly, huge thanks to our former colleagues, Yasmin Ajmal and Guy Shennan, who, over many years, contributed to the discussions, debates and arguments that helped shape the ideas presented in this book.

Introduction

The beginning

In 1986 a group of therapists at the Brief Family Therapy Center in Milwaukee published a paper outlining the beginning of a new and revolutionary way of working (de Shazer et al., 1986). The team, led by Steve de Shazer and Insoo Kim Berg, drew on a range of sources including family therapy, the hypnotherapy of Milton Erickson, Buddhism and the work of philosopher Ludwig Wittgenstein to develop an approach to problem solving that turned traditional thinking on its head.

It is difficult to overestimate the radical significance of the changes that have flowed from de Shazer's reformulation of the accepted truths upon which most therapeutic endeavours had been based until that time. Therapists had generally assumed that they needed to know the nature of the problem that the client brought to therapy, and indeed to understand something of that problem in order for therapy to be effective. Challenging this idea, de Shazer asserted, instead, that the therapist needed only to focus, firstly, on discovering how the client would know the problem had been solved and, secondly, on what they were already doing about it. The therapeutic process that had typically been constructed as a moving *away* from the problem is reconstructed by de Shazer as a process of moving *towards* the solution. This fundamentally called into question the nature of the therapist's expertise, much of which had traditionally been based upon a claimed ability to understand what was

causing problems in the client's life. The professional therapist 'saw' beyond the surface presentation to a hidden world
concealed from the eyes of the untrained. It was this claim to
esoteric knowledge, not available to the layperson or client,
which represented a large part of the therapist's claim to
professional status.

A further challenge to the received wisdom of the time,
and indeed, to the assumptions that most clients have about
the therapeutic process, related to the focus of the therapeutic conversation. In the past it had been assumed that the
greater part of the talking that client and therapist did
together should relate to the problem. Even when the therapist was not trying to understand the cause of a problem it
was assumed that it was somehow good for the client to talk
about it, 'vent' and unburden in order to move on. The usefulness of such 'problem-talk' as de Shazer and his team
described it (Lipchik and de Shazer, 1986) was challenged.
Instead the Milwaukee team proposed that change is
more easily brought about by maximising what they termed
'solution-talk', which they defined as talk that involved a
focus on the client's goals, the client's resources and what
the client was already doing that was working. This proposition was to transform the nature of the talking that goes on
between the client and the therapist, challenging the therapist to develop a whole new repertoire of techniques to
support a radically changed focus.

Another idea that echoed way beyond Milwaukee and
whose ripples are still spreading related to the idea of 'resistance', the idea that therapy can be framed as a struggle
between the therapist, on the side of change, and the client,
whose unspoken agenda is to keep things the same. de Shazer
chose to assume that clients genuinely want to make the
changes that they describe and he reframed all the behaviours that are typically grouped together within the description 'resistance', as the client's unique way of cooperating
(de Shazer, 1984), thereby challenging the therapist to come
closer to the client's frame of reference. By placing the onus
on the therapist to find a way of adjusting to, and fitting with
the client's response, whatever that might have been, de
Shazer called into question another of the fundamental

premises upon which the therapeutic relationship had been constructed.

From problem to solution

These simple, and yet radical, ideas led to the development of a therapy that has challenged many long-held beliefs about the therapeutic process (George, Iveson and Ratner, 1999). Rather than trying to understand and fix problems solution focused brief therapy works by exploring, in detail, a client's preferred future, a description of a time when the problem is solved, and then identifying whatever it is that the client is already doing that fits with the attaining of that future. Thousands of successful cases, many of which have involved clients hitherto seen as untreatable, have confirmed the belief that everyone has a potentially different future and everyone has resources.

The essence of solution focused brief therapy, and solution focused coaching, is therefore:

- to look for resources rather than deficits;
- to explore possible and preferred futures;
- to explore what is already contributing to those futures;
- and to treat clients as the experts in all aspects of their lives.

From therapy to coaching

The shift from a model of therapy to a model of coaching was initially a gradual process. Work is a large part of many people's lives so it was inevitable that relationships and progress at work would be part of many 'therapeutic' conversations. Sometimes a person would have heard about BRIEF on the grapevine and come along specifically for a work-related issue. To the 'therapist' there would be no distinction: work or life, the conversational process is the same.

The second influence on the shift to coaching was the professional advancement of practitioners who had trained in the solution focused approach who were finding their therapy skills useful in other areas, especially management. They began asking for solution focused training more related to their current responsibilities especially in relation to staff supervision and development. Anecdotal evidence suggested that solution focused practice was transferable to many aspects of the manager's role.

The third influence was simply the growth of coaching as part of the support structure for senior staff, based on the realisation that in every company the most valuable resource is the staff team. Organisations that supported, valued and acknowledged the contributions of their staff were being identified by research as the most likely to survive and indeed to prosper in an increasingly competitive global economy (Buckingham and Coffman, 1999). Coaching, it was realised, could deliver benefits not just in terms of work satisfaction, but also in terms of productivity and workforce stability. Coaching was in the marketplace.

However, the success of the new product is evidenced by the extent to which it has now spread beyond the confines of the workplace. Life coaching, couple coaching and parent coaching are all examples of the spread of coaching into worlds previously the domain of counsellors and therapists. That success has been based largely on the extent to which coaches have differentiated themselves from their competitors. Whereas therapy and counselling have been inextricably tied to the idea of problems, to difficulties, to limitations and to some extent have become stigmatised and stigmatising activities associated with failure, coaching has hitched itself to a quite different wagon, to ideas of increased performance, to new futures, to an essentially optimistic world view that believes that all of us could perform better, that all of us have potential that is currently being unrealised. Indeed at times the marketing of coaching appears to suggest that not only could all of us perform better but that it is a new moral imperative, a duty to make the most of the possibilities that are open to us. The differentiation from therapy has been crucial to coaching's success and yet when examined in detail how much evidence is there to justify the claims upon which the field has progressed? How different has coaching been from the approaches to personal change that have preceded it and what difference is there between solution focused coaching and other coaching models and approaches that have already found acceptance in the field?

What's the difference?

At first sight there is not much difference between the broad brushstroke descriptions of solution focused coaching and any other coaching model. Each purports to be future focused and to eschew the exploration of problems. The aim of coaching is to help the client 'grow' rather than solve their problems.

However, on closer inspection, especially with the eyes of a therapist, the similarities between most coaching models and therapy models are striking. The same psychological theories and associated problem-solving methods are lying, barely concealed, just beneath the surface. The fundamental ideas that shape the therapist's relationship with the client emerge just as clearly in much of the writing that describes the coach's interaction with the coachee.

Bruce Peltier (2009) is explicit in his identification of potentially useful models of therapy that can form the basis, in his view, of successful styles of coaching. James Flaherty (1999) is less explicit although he relies heavily on the principles of cognitive behaviour therapy, which is fundamentally problem focused in its way of approaching the difficulties that clients bring. Julie Starr (2003) adamantly claims that coaching is not a problem-solving process yet much of her description of what she does is problem identification (diagnosis in therapy) and problem solving. And the GROW (Goals, Reality, Options, Will) model (Whitmore, 1996) devotes considerable attention to identifying and resolving blocks to progress, again, not a million miles away from diagnosis. What all these, and most other coaching models have at their heart is the notion of 'assessment' and each in its own way sees accurate assessment as the way to effective coaching. It is this that places coaching alongside traditional therapy because to carry out an assessment the coach needs a way to make sense of what is going on in the client's life and needs a way, in order to do this, to decide what data is relevant to collect. What they turn to is psychological theory (cognitive, systemic, learning, psychoanalytic or whatever) and although it may be used less explicitly than in therapy it will still be what helps shape the conversation.

This essential problem focus within so much coaching is in part hidden by the difference in starting points between coaching and therapy. A therapist is likely to ask 'What brings you here?' as an invitation to the client to describe the problem and its history whereas the coach is likely to ask 'What do you want to achieve as a result of coming here?' which is an invitation to talk about goals and the future.

It is when the coach starts the assessment process that they will inevitably be drawn towards problems and at the point in their work when they start to analyse blocks and pitfalls there will be little to distinguish their conversations from the sorts of conversations a therapist might have. This would be less of an issue if block-related conversations were not such a significant part of the whole process. Much coaching has been unable to resist the fascination of focusing on the question 'What is it that is stopping this person fulfilling their potential?' Once coaches go down this assessment route and once they see their task as helping their clients overcome the blocks to progress they will, in the most fundamental way, be acting like therapists however much they might choose to ignore this fact. Even Whitmore in his seminal work *Coaching for Performance* (Whitmore, 1996: 67) states: 'That is the nature of coaching: it addresses cause, not only symptom'. Whitmore goes on to give an example in which he carefully analyses the problematic eating habits of his client thus demonstrating an approach that owes more to traditional therapy, identifying and fixing problems, than he cares to admit.

Solution focused therapy and solution focused coaching

If there is a somewhat disguised similarity between most coaching models and therapy the opposite could be said of the relationship between solution focused coaching and its therapeutic counterpart: they are virtually indistinguishable and happily so. There is no question that might be asked in a coaching session that would not be equally at home in a therapy session and vice versa. This does not mean that all sessions are identical but rather coaching and therapy sessions follow the same principles and would almost always start with the same question. The only discernable and to some extent predictable difference would be in the first answer: a coaching client is more likely to see the purpose of the session in terms of a positive outcome such as being more focused at work or completing a particular task whereas a client for therapy will be more prone to begin by seeking a negative outcome such as the eradication of a problem. However, within a question or two, as the examples below illustrate transcripts of the two sessions will have no marked difference other than content; they will both follow the same process.

Harold was a very successful, very senior executive who was contemplating a career change and becoming a coach so had come for a 'taste'.

Coach: So, Harold, what are your best hopes from this session?

Harold: It might seem a bit strange, Chris, because I have always been seen as a very confident person and obviously to a degree I must be because of what I have achieved but the thing is I don't always feel confident, so that's what I'd like, I'd like to feel more confidence.

Coach: What difference do you think that would make?

Harold: A very big difference!

Carol was referred by a community mental health team specialising in patients with 'severe and enduring mental illness'.

Coach: So, Carol, what are your best hopes from this session?

Carol: I don't know really. I'm not sure. I've suffered from severe depression all my adult life so I suppose if you could do something about that. I'd like not to be depressed all the time.

Coach: What would you want to replace it – replace the depression.

Carol: I'd like to feel more confident.
Coach: What difference do you think that would make?
Carol: A very big difference!

From this point on in each session there will be no need for the coach to refer to depression or 'lack of confidence' again; each session will follow a similar path even as each client describes a different path.

Since its origins in the mid-1980s solution focused practice has been evolving in many different directions. Some versions will be closer to the GROW model with its emphasis on planning and targets (O'Connell, 2001), some are closer to neurolinguistic programming using techniques drawn from hypnosis (O'Hanlon and Martin, 1992), some will be very task oriented (Berg and Miller, 1992) and some will be hybrids of solution focus and other models (McFarland,1995). The BRIEF version has attempted to follow the principle of Ockham's Razor, advocated by de Shazer, that what can be achieved by fewer means should not be achieved by many. This requires the constant examination of assumptions and a preparedness to abandon even the most sacred of cows if a desired outcome can be achieved without them. As will be seen in later chapters this has led us to some remarkable discoveries about the process of change.

Others have also developed their own models of solution focused coaching, including Berg and Szabo (2005), Jackson and McKergow (2002) and Pemberton (2006) but what is distinctive about the BRIEF approach is the extent to which everything is left to the client who is seen as the only expert in his or her life. Every attempt is made to eliminate any direct intentionality on the part of the coach. What the client does after the session is only the client's business, all the coach has done if she has been successful is, through the conversational process, help the client see more possibilities and choices. What choice the client makes is not the coach's concern. This was not an easy point to arrive at since the coach's livelihood is dependent on the client making 'good' choices. Fortunately, although we cannot say that this 'hands off' position has led to improved outcomes, we can say that we achieve the same outcomes in fewer sessions. A lesson we have learned (again) from this is that trust pays: trusting the client to make his own best decision leads to the decision being made sooner.

Conclusion

The model described in this book will pose a serious challenge to many current coaching practices. It will also offer some intriguing possibilities that are not only likely to make coaching sessions more economical but will also increase the sense of satisfaction of both coach and client. The danger is that the model will be seen as too simplistic or even banal. It is neither: simple, yes; simplistic, no. Concerned with the routine and humdrum, yes; banal no more than life is banal. Just a quick dip into any of the transcripts is likely to reveal some apparently trivial aspect of the client's life and as far as the solution focused coach is concerned this is how it should be. The model has been developed with clients facing major life- and future-threatening problems: suicidal depression, drug addiction, school exclusion, family breakdown and has been as successful as any other therapy model. Its failure to provide a diagnostic framework, to address problems (rather than develop solutions) has prevented its more widespread acceptance in the medical model dominated health and social services. However, in the world of coaching, it offers a genuinely problem-free framework for constructing creative conversations and thus achieves what many other models still aspire towards.

Summary

- Steve de Shazer and the team at the Milwaukee Brief Family Therapy Center developed a model of therapy that challenged many of the underpinning assumptions of the traditional therapy world.
- Although asserting its difference from therapy, coaching has in fact drawn on many ideas directly derived from the world of therapy, in particular in its interest in making sense of what is keeping the client stuck and what the client might therefore need to change.

- Solution focused coaching and solution focused therapy are virtually indistinguishable.
- Even within the solution focused arena there are different models. Of all of these BRIEF's model is the least interventive and the briefest.

Activity

This is a simple (although not necessarily easy) self-supervising procedure for when a coach begins to experience an impasse with a client. It will also illustrate in a practical way the creative impact of a disciplined focus on resources.

Focusing on resources

- Think of a client with whom you are feeling stuck, despondent or even a little bit hopeless.
- Instead of trying to analyse the stuckness (yours or the client's) take a pen and paper and spend 10 minutes listing at least twenty specific strengths and resources that your client might lay claim to.
- Read through the list just prior to your next session.
- Notice the difference.

2

Basic principles

Rules of conversation

Solution focused coaching is a conversational process and as we have all been learning conversational skills from birth we are all familiar with the basic rules. These rules tend only to be noticed when they are broken. The two enemies of conversation are interruption and non-sequiters. Both in their different ways block the creative flow of conversation by breaking one of two basic rules. The first breaks the rule of turn taking and the second breaks the rule of circularity.

The vast majority of our learning, about ourselves, about the world and about our work, comes from conversation. It is the process by which we define and grow to understand the world and our part in it. If we don't talk we start to disappear. We all experience social situations where for one reason or another we can't find our voice and often feel diminished as a result. Speaking in social situations gives us a part in defining those situations and thus, at that moment, in helping to define the world we live in. If we don't have a voice the world is defined by others and ultimately we lose our place often with disastrous consequences not just for us but for society more generally.

The conversational rule of turn taking ensures that in any social situation there is an equality of opportunity to contribute to how that situation evolves, to how that small corner of the world is created. If the rule is broken then some people take more than their own turn and therefore exert more influence at the expense of others. The formal and informal power structures of any organisation can be traced by following the voices of those who speak in gatherings, and in particular those who set and control the conversational agenda, whether in a board meeting or at the pub after work.

Although there are some formal gatherings where it is necessary and legitimate for certain people's voices to be heard more than others these are few compared with our conversational life in total, even our conversational life at work. If someone regularly experiences an apparent inability to speak at work it could be that they are being routinely interrupted (or ignored). If this is being done purposefully then it begins to fall into the realm of workplace bullying and becomes a danger to all involved. Jack Welch the former chief executive officer (CEO) of General Electric commented 'In an environment where we must have every good idea from every man and woman in the organisation we cannot afford management styles that suppress and intimidate' (cited in Nicholas, 2008: 330). Within these terms turn taking is seen as necessary for an organisation's survival.

The creativity of conversation is ensured by the rule of circularity. In a true conversation each contribution builds on the last. This, ultimately, is how we know that we are being listened to: when the other person says something that connects with and develops what we have just said. Everything else to do with listening can be faked! The creative process occurs because I have an idea which leads you to an idea made up of mine and your independent reaction to it. I react to your development of my idea and as we progress we develop an understanding that neither of us could have had on our own but that fits us both perfectly even though we might not have exactly the same idea of what it actually means.

Every conversation that follows these two rules will have a creative potential whether its subject is a computer glitch or the coming home time of a teenager. Just as we instantly recognise interruptions we instantly recognise breaches of the circularity rule and where possible we avoid those who regularly ignore these rules.

Given the almost inevitable creativity of true conversation any coach who follows these rules to the letter is likely to have some success. The conversation will create new meanings and new understandings and from these might spring new behaviour. As Ludwig Fleck the Polish biologist points out 'He is a poor observer who does not notice that a stimulating conversation between two persons soon creates a condition in which each utters thoughts he would not have been able to produce by himself or in different company' (cited in Miller and de Shazer, 1998: 364).

Professional conversations

Whereas social conversations need no specific purpose other than helping to keep us in the world, professional conversations take place for a specific purpose that is contracted between the professional and the client. We will talk about this process of contracting later. Different rules govern these conversations one of them being that the professional should seek no more knowledge about the client than is necessary for the job in hand. If the purpose of collecting any information is unclear we are likely to challenge and to withhold the information if there is no good reason given. (We have all asked a service provider questions like 'Why do you want to know where I went to school?' and been reassured by the answer 'For security so we can ask you when you phone us'. The information has a purpose related to our contract with the provider.) In these professional conversations the professional's task is to manage the conversation in order to reach the desired outcome. Seeking more information than is necessary can be deemed intrusive or, as Bill O'Hanlon (2001) has suggested can be seen as the professional 'sight-seeing in the client's life', an interesting journey, maybe, but not the most direct nor the most cost-effective.

Coaching is at the most complex end of the spectrum of professional conversations but it is still the coach's responsibility to manage the conversation in a way that produces the desired result. This means that the coach not only has to follow the two basic rules, turn taking and circularity, but also has to have a way of deciding what aspect of each of the client's responses to take up in the next conversational turn. And because the client has the right at any point to ask 'Why do you need to know that?' the coach must be aware of the choices he is making each time he asks a question. Given the multiplicity of possible responses to what the client last said the coach needs a way of filtering and processing the information and this is the main purpose of a coaching model. It gives us a way of processing what the client says and deciding to which parts to respond.

Elective listening

In any conversation we have to make choices about what part of the other person's contribution to build on. An opening question 'Have you come far?' might elicit the response: 'No, only from round the corner today though it did take me longer than I expected'. In responding to this simple, unexceptional answer there are nonetheless a host of possibilities. The coach might enquire where the client came from, whether a longer journey had been made yesterday, about the time that the journey had taken or the mode of transport or, most likely, about why the journey had taken longer than expected. As long as the response picked up one aspect of the answer then listening would have been demonstrated. However, each response would also take the conversation in a different direction. The more complex the conversation is the greater the number of entirely unknown possibilities that the conversation holds.

In social conversations the choice is a constant negotiation and renegotiation with an equally shared responsibility for the overall process. In professional conversations the professional's choice of response is guided by the agreed purpose and the professional's method of achieving that purpose. For some this will involve gathering certain sorts of information, often about problems (or blocks to action) from which to make a judgement about possible remedies and for others, including the solution focused coach, it will involve invitations to clients to describe certain aspects of their lives, past, present and (hypothetically) future that the coach assumes to be associated with a greater likelihood of progress. In each case the professional will listen carefully to the client's response and select from it the stepping stone that is likely to lead to the next question that best supports the possibility of progress.

Coach: So what have you done in the past that worked?

Client: I did once take it up with him and things were different for a while but it didn't last long. He was soon back to his old ways. In fact, I sometimes think he got worse after that; he certainly seemed to send more of his critical emails and I think that's what really got to me in the end; I just dreaded going into work knowing there'll probably be another insinuating email. It's not just me. I know other people find him difficult. I don't know how they put up with it. It certainly doesn't seem to affect the others so much. I don't know what I'm going to do but I'm certain that I can't go on like this because it is having a really serious effect on my home life and if he ends up destroying my marriage – it's just terrible, I can't go on like this!

In this sequence the coach listens to everything the client says and then must choose which part of the client's answer to follow. Different models will point to different questions. Many will try to 'get to the bottom' of the problem:

- 'Why do you think it didn't last?'
- 'What is it that you actually dread?'
- 'What exactly is he doing and in what ways is it worse?'
- 'What do other people find difficult?'
- 'Why do others find him less difficult than you do?'
- 'Why do you find him more difficult than they do?'
- 'What effect is it having on your marriage?'

These 'finding out' questions are part of the coach's attempt to understand what is going on including, towards the latter part of the list, the possibility that the 'real' problem might be the client. It would not stretch imagination too far to see this line of questions leading to a referral on for 'therapy'.

The solution focused coach would choose to hear that part of the answer that referred to a past success:

Coach: I can see why you would want to do something about it! So tell me more about taking it up with him. How did you manage to do that even though it didn't improve things for long?

This question acknowledges the extent of the difficulties and builds the next question on the part of the answer that seems most likely to lead to a successful resolution because anything that can last a short time can last longer. All the information about the problem: the nature of the difficulty, the criticisms, the fear and dread, the effect on the marriage is only responded to in the most general terms as the professional acknowledges the client's good reasons for wanting things to change. Making purposeful and directional choices is a fundamental part of the professional conversation and it is the coach's theory that will help him decide which part of the client's response to pick up and which to let go by. Knowing what to let go by is just as important a skill as knowing upon which elements of the client's response to construct the next question.

Meeting the person

In many cultures business is rarely commenced without some preliminary social talk usually unrelated to the purpose of the meeting. We in the West often mistake this practice as a waste of time or unnecessary. What we have forgotten in our role-defined lives is that business between two people is best conducted person-to-person and not role-to-role. The function of a social period before the hard business talk begins is to allow the two *persons* to meet because it is thought that both are then more likely to be satisfied with the deal that is eventually struck.

This is a practice most coaches will be familiar with although they may do it for different reasons. In solution focused work meeting the person (rather than the role of client) is essential because it is the person of the client who holds the wherewithal for a successful outcome. Social talk is not therefore a 'softening up', nor a 'rapport-building' process, even though it may have a rapport-building effect, but a way for client and coach to meet person-to-person before getting down to business.

The guideline here is: for a few minutes to talk about anything *except* the issue that brings the client to you. This will inevitably create a freer-flowing conversation that quite incidentally might prove helpful further on in the meeting. During this social talk a client recently spoke of his involvement in his son's school as a governor during a time of change. Later this proved a useful and successful parallel to an issue he was struggling with at work.

The frame for these initial conversations is to assume that the client is an interesting competent equal who is likely, during the course of the meeting, to generate useful thoughts that will lead to productive actions whether or not the coach or client knows what these thoughts and actions might be until they happen. Coaches will be more familiar with the assumption of client competence than therapists unfamiliar with the work of Daniel Gassman and Klaus Grawe (2006: 10) whose research in the field of therapy established that: '[Successful therapists] created an environment in which the patient felt he was perceived as a well functioning person. As soon as this was established, productive work on the patient's problems was more likely'. This social talk period will help to establish and acknowledge the client's well-functioning status and thereby bring even their hidden resources closer to the surface to be more available for problem solving. If the client does not cooperate with this way of starting it is the solution focused coach's task to cooperate with the client's preferences. There may be many reasons why a client will be uncomfortable with an initial social phase: they may think time is money and this is not time well spent; they may feel 'coerced' into coaching and therefore not respond to such a 'friendly' approach; they may for whatever reason be too tense to begin in a relaxed way; and they may want to say what they have to say as soon as possible, to get it off their chest. Whatever the reason, as soon as the coach realises that social talk is cutting across the client's preferred way of proceeding he needs to change tack and one way or another get down to business.

Listening with a constructive ear

Sometimes a client will start immediately with an account of their circumstances. This is most likely to happen if the coaching has been arranged in response to some difficulties in the person's work life. It may be possible to interrupt just to do whatever scene setting a coach might prefer but if a client begins like this he is likely to continue describing the difficulty as soon as possible and the solution focused coach will then listen, but do so with a 'constructive ear' (Lipchik, 1988). One way to jointly manage this aspect of a session is to ask the client how much of the time they want to use to describe the situation and how much they want to leave for finding the best way forward. This allows the coach to manage the session while the client stays in control of its shape and content.

It is important to remember that being solution focused is not the same as being problem phobic. Clients are free to talk about whatever they want to talk about. What the solution focused coach must do is listen with a constructive ear. This means listening to build rather than listening to understand. When we try to understand the problem and the client's part in it we cannot fail to do so in the light of a theory of human behaviour however implicit or even unacknowledged that theory is. There is also a real risk that our theory will direct us to what is going wrong and from there it is only a short step wondering what might be the client's part in the problem. This, in turn, will take us to the client's deficits and limitations.

Clients, however, do not usually resolve their problems by drawing on their deficits. They resolve them by drawing on their resources. However skilful, sensitive, committed and appropriate our work with clients may be we cannot *make* clients change. Clients will ultimately either change or not change depending on the resources upon which they can draw. It is the client, in the end, who will either use our work with them or not and in using it, the client will, in the most general sense, be drawing on their capacity to change, a capacity that will itself draw on a range of personal resources. If we assume that our clients *do not* have the resources required to resolve the issues that they bring, then generally coaching will confirm that assumption. If on the other hand we assume that our clients *do* have the resources required to resolve the problems that they bring, then again generally coaching will confirm that assumption. Sometimes, in the process, clients, will discover resources that they (and we) knew nothing about.

It is the aim of solution focused interviewing to help clients to *notice* and to *describe* what they do that is useful for them. This 'noticing and describing' will depend on the coach's capacity for constructive listening; hearing elements in a flow of conversation to which it might be useful to draw the client's attention by asking a question. The subsequent noticing on the part of the client will then lead to a greater sense of personal agency. Typical questions that elicit the client's resources range from the simple and straightforward:

- 'How did you do that?'
- 'How did you get through that time/experience/deal with that difficulty?'

to slightly more complex, inclusive questions such as:

- 'How did you keep yourself going despite feeling bullied?'
- 'How did you manage to lead that process in the department so well despite feeling that you lacked the experience?'
- 'What did you do to find the strength to challenge him despite his reputation?'

These questions can be called *strategy* questions in the sense that they help to define useful strategies and actions on the part of the client while at the same time inviting the client to take ownership of the achievement. Then there are questions that invite the client to translate actions into meanings and to develop new meanings about the sort of person they might be. These can be described as *identity* questions:

- 'What did it take to do that?'
- 'What did you learn about yourself by managing to do that?'
- 'What sort of conclusions do you imagine that others might have reached about the sort of person that you can be as they observed you handling that situation so well?'

In this way solution focused coaching aims to create a context within which the client gives himself affirmative feedback that in turn builds new possibilities for the client's future.

Clients are far more likely to accept their own positive descriptions than positive feedback given by others. By listening with a constructive ear, listening for the alternative or unspoken version of a problem description, the coach is able to construct questions that lead the client towards self-affirming answers. This is very different from pointing out positives to clients, trying to get them to see their strengths and giving them praise! Occasionally the frustrated coach can be heard to say 'I just can't get her to see her own strengths', a clear indication, however benevolently intended, that the coach is telling rather than asking and even beginning to argue with the client. Solution focus works through asking questions each of which creates an opportunity for the client to hear himself articulating a new and different thought. Each and any of these 'articulations' might be the news from which a different future is envisaged. Whatever coaching model is used real and lasting change will only occur when the client sees and does something different.

Constructive listening acutely sensitises the coach to listen for the client's competencies, qualities and abilities so even in the most problem-saturated accounts the coach will ask questions which invite the client to consider a more positive and enabling self-view. This in itself is likely to make a difference. However, constructive listening also impacts on the coach's responses to the client, building in the coach an expectation that the outcome for the piece of work will indeed be good, an expectation that is conveyed to the client through the minute details of the coach's responses in the session that are beyond conscious control, such as voice tone, phraseology, body posture and eye contact. Christophe Flückiger and Martin Grosse Holtforth's (2008) research is one of many accounts demonstrating the connection between awareness of resource and positive outcome. They invited a group of trainee psychologists to spend 5 minutes before and after a series of client sessions discussing with a colleague their client's strengths. On completion and when compared with the work of similar trainees who had not gone through the same process, they found that these particular trainees achieved better relationships with the client, as judged from video-taped recordings, and better outcomes.

If you heard that story on Woman's Hour

Patrick had a glittering record of academic, sporting and artistic achievement but left Oxbridge just before his finals. Declining counselling he agreed to see a coach to talk about career possibilities. Although Patrick decided to complete his studies the crisis had thrown his mother into a self-critical crisis of her own and a few weeks later asked for career coaching on her own behalf. Maria and her husband had both had very successful careers in their home country. When their children were still small a change of regime led to their departure, not through necessity but by choice; they did not want their children to grow up in what they considered to be an unjust society. Settling in a new country with little money, few possessions and no recognition of their former professions they began again and within not many years had rebuilt their careers and their wealth. Then new laws in their adopted country led them to move again, this time to Britain. Once again a fresh start was required but this time Maria's husband suffered a mental and physical collapse. Unhappy with his medical treatment she had begun an investigation herself, successfully treated her husband and was about to publish a groundbreaking book on the condition. Maria presented as an abject failure seeing her decision to move from country to country for essentially selfish reasons as the cause of her husband's ill health, her children's instability and the family's relative poverty. The account took around 20 minutes. The coach then asked Maria if she listened to Woman's Hour (on BBC radio 4), which she did. He then asked, 'If on the way here you'd been listening in the car and heard a woman tell the story that you have just told me, what would you think of her?' Maria thought for several moments and then said quite unequivocally, 'I'd think she was bloody marvellous!' From the position of bad mother and failure Maria could see a long history of self-induced failure that put her whole family's future at risk. From the position of admired woman on the radio she saw a family prepared to stand up and be counted, a family who put social responsibility before personal wealth and a family who could make mistakes and recover.

Throughout this meeting the coach expressed no independent opinion about Maria. Instead he asked questions and followed those answers that seemed most likely to point in the direction of the family's continued success.

Summary

- Solution focused coaching is a conversational process and in common with social conversations it depends on the twin rules of turn taking and circularity.
- The shape of any conversation is constructed through the choices we make about which elements of the other's response to pick up and which to let go by.
- In professional conversations the coach's choice of questions will be guided by the theoretical model used.
- Meeting people person-to-person enhances the likelihood of a relationship based on an acknowledgement of the competence of both parties.
- Solution focus listens with a constructive ear searching for opportunities to invite the client to notice and describe his competences and resources.

Activities: Listening skills

It is easier said than done to listen with a constructive ear. Most people's default position when listening to a person talking about a problem is to try to solve it. This requires us to ask questions about the problem and then to make 'helpful' suggestions which are usually rebuffed by 'Yes, but …'

Activity 1: Delight (or annoy) your friends with reflective listening

Next time a friend tells you about a problem put your problem-solving skills to one side. Brilliant as these skills may be you know in your heart of hearts that they serve more to shine a positive light on you rather than illuminate the problem. Instead, listen for your friend's skills and positive attributes that will be hidden in the story and then give a bit of feedback on these. If your friend wants to hear more ask a few questions about what is it about the situation that gives your friend hope that it can be resolved.

Notice what difference this makes to the quality of the conversation. Then, if you can no longer hold it in, give your advice and hope it will be ignored (because your friend will already have moved on).

Activity 2: Reflexive listening (thanks to Paul Z. Jackson [2006], Amsterdam)

This activity will tie you in knots in the same way that an experienced driver will be confused by carefully noting the techniques of driving rather than just doing it.

One person interview another for 5 minutes about their weekend (or any other easy topic).

The interviewer can ask any question as long as it includes at least one key word from the previous answer. After 5 minutes, or when the chain is broken, change roles.

3

Establishing the contract

Best hopes

Establishing the client's purpose in meeting with a coach marks the beginning of 'business'. Whether this follows a more social 'meet-the-person' interchange or the purpose is asked immediately after the greeting is a matter for the coach to decide just as a shopkeeper might or might not pass the time of day before asking 'How can I help you?' The most common starting question at BRIEF is: 'What are your best hopes from our work together?' This invites the client to talk straight away about *outcome*. It means that we are being careful to establish what the client is commissioning us to help them achieve and thereby centralising the client in the process. There is no assessment procedure in solution focused work, no attempt to establish what, on the basis of our supposed 'expert' knowledge, the client *should* want from us. The solution focused approach is always straightforwardly based on what the *client* wants from the work, not on a professionally generated notion of what the client is deemed, according to the professional's own preferred theories, to 'need'.

Process or outcome

Critical at this point is that the contract established between coach and client, the answer to the 'best hopes' question, needs to specify an *outcome* rather than a *process*. A process response is one that relates to what might happen during the session, or what the client thinks needs to happen outside the session in order to achieve the desired outcome. When the client's first response to the 'best hopes' question is a process response the coach will engage the client in a series of further questions aimed at teasing out the hoped-for outcome.

Coach: What are your best hopes from this meeting?

Client: Just a chance to talk things over. There's no one I can really talk to about this so – yes, just to talk to someone who's not involved.

Coach: And if talking things over turned out to be useful what would you hope it would lead to?

Client: A bit more clarity. There's so much going on and at so many different levels.

Coach: And if you gained more clarity what difference do you hope that would make?

Client: I'd feel like I knew where I was going – I could get on and do things. At the moment I feel paralysed!

Coach: OK. So if this meeting led to more clarity, to you feeling that you know where you are going and can get on and do things, would that mean it had been useful?

Client: Yes. Absolutely. I know there's no easy answers and that there's going to need to be a lot of rethinking so if I could start getting on with it that would be great!

Coach: OK. So the bottom line is 'getting on with it'. If our meeting helps you 'get on with it' it will have been useful?

Accepting the first answer, just to talk, would give no clue about the direction in which the conversation might usefully go and of course no picture of the client's desired outcome, the 'outside coaching', real life difference that the client is hoping for. The coach might have been tempted to ask 'What would you like to talk about?' but this would still have led to an answer that related to the process of the coaching rather than to something outside of that context and might have committed the coach to a direction ('Let me tell you all about the problem') that would have been unhelpful for a solution focused approach.

Notice in this example the outcome is not related to a specific achievement but to what is, in fact, another level of process. However, as this is a 'getting on with life' process it is fair to assume it will lead to multiple positive differences in the client's world that the client will be able to imagine and to describe in concrete and observable terms.

Means and ends

Coach: Well, we've got up to four sessions! What are your best hopes from them? What do you hope to achieve from our meetings?

Client: To be honest I can't see how this is going to help.

Coach: OK. I can appreciate that this wasn't necessarily your idea of the way to go but if, nonetheless, it turned out to be a good decision, what do you hope it might lead to?

Client: My so called colleague would get fired!

Coach: What difference do you hope that would make to you?

Client: It would mean I could come to work without a sense of dread; wake up without a sense of dread! I might even start looking forward to coming to work again and when I got here I wouldn't be looking over my shoulder all the time waiting for him to have a go – I could do the job I'm paid to do *and* am perfectly able to do – if I'm just left alone!

Coach: So if these meetings somehow led you to be able to look forward to coming into work again and to you being able to do the job you are paid to do that would mean it's been useful?

Client: If it could!

In this case the client's initial 'best hope', the firing of a colleague, is not viewed by the coach as an *end* in itself but as a '*means to an end*'. In this sense it is part of the client's imagined process towards a desired outcome. Once this outcome has been specified the client and coach can explore a range of potential pathways, other than merely that specified by the client. In so doing the client can discover significantly more flexibility in the way forward, rather than finding herself tied to a single pathway that may never happen and in relation to which the client may have no influence.

There is no easy way to recognise and make these distinctions: to a large degree it comes from practice and from the experience of contracts which do, or do not, lead to constructive conversations. This will become clearer, though not totally clear, as the book progresses.

Problem description

Another very typical answer to the 'best hopes' question is a description of a problem that invites the coach to make a 'problem eradication' or 'problem-solving' contract. Such contracts do not give sufficient outcome-related information to enable the coach to know in which direction to go. It is a bit like climbing into a cab and responding to the driver's 'Where to?' with 'Away from the airport'. In such circumstances the coach will have a clear idea of what the client does not want (to be at the airport), but no picture at all of what the client might want instead. Progress in such circumstances might turn out to be unnecessarily circuitous and thereby unjustifiably costly. A further danger to the client might be that the coach decides that she herself does know the correct destination and begins to try to move the client in her own preferred direction. Steve de Shazer wrote (1987: 60) 'If you want to get from point A to point B, but know no details of the terrain in between, the best thing to do is assume that you can go from A to B by following a straight line. If that assumption proves faulty and you run into huge mountains, then you need to look for a pass that is as close as possible to your original straight line. As William of Ockham might say, never introduce complex descriptions when simple ones will do'. Without knowledge of the destination finding that straightest line is impossible and in such circumstances it is usually the client who pays the price.

Coach: What are your best hopes from our work together?
Client: I think I'm being bullied.

Coach: So from coming here?
Client: I'd like the bullying to stop.
Coach: And if the bullying stopped what difference do you
         hope that would make?

The answer to this last question is the one from which the
contract will be made.

Finding the 'good reason'

More commonly than might be imagined some clients
will initially 'not know' what they want to achieve as a
result of the coaching. This might be someone who at an
abstract level thought coaching would be a good idea or
it might be someone who in some way feels constrained
to attend. In either case the solution focused coach will
assume:

1 that the client is there for a 'good reason' – a reason that
   makes sense to them; and,
2 that it is the coach's job to elicit this 'good reason'.

In the following example the coach has to work very hard to
find out Michael's 'good reason'. Note how each question
accepts and builds on the preceding answers, how every
question contains the unwavering assumption that Michael
does indeed have a 'good reason' for being there and that by
closely following the logic of Michael's answers a contract is
finally agreed upon. Michael was 'advised' to take up his
company's offer to provide four sessions of coaching. Even
before the session began he had taken issue with BRIEF's
use of unrecycled stationery thus showing himself to be a
person well able to speak his mind!

Coach: So what are your best hopes from these meetings?
Client: I don't know.
Coach: So what do you think – what do you think your best
         hopes are?
Client: I've no idea.
Coach: Yet here you are.
Client: Yeah!
Coach: So how come you are here?

Client: Because I was sent.

Coach: So it's not your idea of a good idea?

Client: No it isn't.

Coach: Yet you still decided to come?

Client: I told you! I was told to come.

Coach: Look, I scarcely know you but you do not seem to me to be a person who unthinkingly does as he's told! In fact, you come over as a person with strong views who isn't afraid to share them!

Client: Yeah, well.

Coach: So how come you decided to agree to come?

Client: Because I was told I could lose my job if I didn't.

Coach: OK, that makes sense. And you want to keep your job?

Client: No! I hate it. I'd give it up tomorrow if I could!

Coach: And would that be a good move or . . .?

Client: I'd go if I could but where am I going to get another job that pays this well at my age?

Coach: OK, so even though you don't like the job you can't afford to lose it?

Client: No I can't.

Coach: So if these meetings help you keep the job, in a way that is right for you, would that mean they had been useful?

Client: These meetings won't do anything. It's all talk. They just want me to say 'yes, sir, no, sir; anything you say, sir!'

Coach: Which wouldn't be your style at all.

Client: *(Humph!)*

Coach: I'm not saying these meetings will be any use but if they did lead to you finding a way not only to keep your job but to keep it in a way that is also right for you personally would that mean they had been useful?

Client: I suppose so but I don't see how they will.

Coach: Well I guess we've got nothing to lose so shall we give it a try? It will mean me asking you a lot of hard questions.

Client: OK, go on then.

The common project

Harry Korman (Korman, 2004) clarifies the issues involved in contracting, which he calls establishing a 'common project'. Korman proposes that the common project has three elements and that each must be fulfilled if we are to enhance the prospect of a successful outcome.

1 The contract must represent something that the client wants to achieve or to change in his life.
2 The thing that the client wants to change or to achieve must be something that fits within the legitimate remit of the coach.
3 The thing that the client wants to change or to achieve must be something that the coach and client working well together could hope to achieve.

Failure to fit with these three core conditions jeopardises the likely good outcome of the work.

A preferred outcome must represent something that the client wants to achieve or to change in his life

The first of the common contractual conditions initially seems less than problematic. How difficult could it be to figure out what the client wants to change or to achieve? Yet, as in the examples above, this can indeed present an issue to the coach. It has often been said that 'I don't know' is the most common answer offered by clients in relation to any question. Sometimes of course this response is indeed no more than a verbal tic, a habitual way of responding that means very little at all. However, when the client answers 'I don't know', not just at the 'first fence' but in response to a series of questions it can have a number of meanings and it is likely to be useful to the coach to reflect on which of these seems most likely.

- Sometimes 'I don't know' is just a way to create thinking time and if the coach remains silent the client will then begin to answer more constructively.
- Sometimes the client is expecting a different question, like 'What brings you here?' and has prepared an 'explanation' but has not articulated a desired outcome. The

coach's pause, if it does not lead to an answer might be followed by 'What do you think?' or even 'have a guess'.

- When this leads nowhere useful it may just mean that the client has not quite understood the question in which case rephrasing can often break the deadlock: 'If coming here turned out to be useful what difference would you hope it will make?'
- Seeking the perspective of an interested third party might also provide a lead into the contract: 'How would your closest colleague/partner/best friend know that coming here had been useful to you? What might they see that would tell them?'
- And sometimes, because the client has been 'sent', he or she is less inclined to buy into a contract. In such cases an acknowledgement of this difficulty can be the beginning of a productive conversation as in the following example.

Coach: I am beginning to get the idea that it was not your idea to come and meet with me today.

Client: No it was not.

Coach: So whose idea was it?

Client: My boss's.

Coach: So what are your boss's best hopes for this? How could she know that your meeting with me has ended up making a difference?

Client: Well she wants me to be more assertive and feels that I have problems with this.

Coach: So would it be good for you if she were to stop having this idea about you?

Client: Yes I guess. Yes it would, because at the moment she feels that this is holding me back so I am not getting the opportunities that some of the others are getting.

Coach: OK so how would she know that you were being assertive in the right way so that she won't feel that she needs to worry about you and you get the opportunities that you want?

At this point coach and client are on the verge of agreeing a 'common project' which will be of benefit to the client and which also fits with the best hopes of the referrer, namely demonstrating to the client's boss that the client has the capacity to be assertive in order that the client can get what the client wants, namely more opportunities. The client is now engaging in the process and will remain engaged as long as the coach remembers that the contract for the work is based on the client getting opportunities and that assertiveness is merely a route to that end. If the coach begins to believe, and therefore to communicate to the client the idea that she believes that the client needs to be more assertive, then she risks eliciting the same response as the client's manager has experienced, namely self-protective withdrawal. However, while the coach's focus remains firmly on how the client can get the opportunities that he feels that he deserves, then the client is likely to work well.

A preferred outcome must be something that fits within the legitimate remit of the coach

Establishing that the desired change fits within the coach's legitimate remit is usually simple and straightforward, although care does need to be paid to the question who is paying for the service and if the payment is coming from an employer, what range of issues it is legitimate to address. Negotiating the boundary between coaching, which the employer may wish to fund, and counselling or therapy, which the employer may not wish to pay for, might at times require reflection. Treading this particular boundary may also raise the question 'Am I qualified to deal with the issues that this client is raising or should I be seeking someone with the relevant training and experience?' By and large however, the legitimacy of the client's desired changes in relation to the coach's role is relatively unproblematic.

A preferred outcome must also be something that the coach and client working well together could hope to achieve

The third of Korman's criteria relates to feasibility. How likely is the specified change to be achieved should the client and coach work well together? Some clients, with striking ambition can set themselves daunting targets: 'Well I'll know that this has been useful if I'm confidently on track towards being

CEO of this organisation'. The solution focused coach can normally negotiate good enough fit with such energetic and aspiring clients by focusing on the first signs that the client is on track towards her ultimate ambition and working with the client until the path is sufficiently well established. 'Let's imagine that from this point on your career moves in exactly the direction you hope: what's the first thing your colleagues will notice about you as you walk into your office tomorrow?'

More challenging are those clients whose 'best hopes' involve changing another's behaviour or attitude whether that be 'he'll be off my back', 'she'll recognise my talents', 'she'll stop being so rude' or 'she'll want to cooperate with me instead of fighting me all the time'. In these circumstances the track that the solution focused coach takes depends on the client's answer to the question 'and how likely do you think it is that the other will change?' If the client responds with 'not at all likely – he's always been like this and I cannot imagine him changing now', the coach will ask 'OK then – so what *are* your best hopes as a result of coming here?' The client's initial 'best hopes' have just been defined (by the client) as highly unlikely and therefore cannot form the basis for a common contract. Very often the client will then highlight a wish to find ways of coping better with the other's behaviour and the coping with the other will become the basis for the common contract. On other occasions the client responds by saying that she does believe that the desired change in the other can happen. The coach can enquire about the client's evidence for this 'so what gives you the idea that this can happen' and if the client remains convinced the coach can accept this as the basis for the work. The capacity of a solution focused conversation to create change in others will be looked at more closely in a later chapter.

Summary

- The solution focused approach is non-normative in the sense that it has no way of knowing how people should be, no way of determining what the client should be working towards. It therefore depends for its commission on the client specifying what he wants.

- The solution focused practitioner seeks to establish with the client a 'common contract'.
- The contract will typically represent an outcome, a difference in the client's world rather than a process response that relates to the coaching itself.
- The contract will also typically be an end in itself rather than a means to an end.

Activities: Contracting

Activity 1 'Don't know'

Fill in the coach's responses in the following sequence making sure that each response accepts, validates (overtly or tacitly) and builds on the client's previous answer.

Coach: What are your best hopes from our meeting today?
Client: I don't know.
Coach: ....
Client: I don't know.
Coach: ....
Client: I don't know.
Coach: ....
Client: I don't know.
Coach: ....

And as long as you can manage!
Try this several times either on your own writing down the questions or with a partner or group in a role play. The key is to carry the impregnable assumption that the client is there for a very good and logical reason and that if you get the question right the client will reveal it. Making statements is usually unhelpful unless they are tentative compliments to the client.

The more times you try it the more you will look forward to your next 'Don't know' answer.

Activity 2: What makes a good contract

- In a small group rotate the turns to be coach and client until everyone has had at least one chance to be both.

- The coach's task is to begin the process of establishing a working contract – a hoped-for destination for the coaching journey.
- Each turn should last no more than 3 minutes and in some the contract will have been achieved well within that time whereas in others it will still be some way off.
- When everyone has taken a turn at both roles discuss.

This is an exercise that can be repeated over and over. Even the most experienced brief coaches will learn from it.

4

Preferred futures

Once the contract has been made the solution focused coach has two tasks:

1 to help the client describe what will be different in their hoped-for future; and
2 to describe what they might already be doing or have done in the past that could in some way help bring their preferred future to life.

Where the coach invites the client to focus first is not necessarily a matter of crucial significance. What matters is the degree of detail achieved. A client might express a wish to be a more effective chairman; the coach could begin by asking 'What are the ways you are doing a good job already?' and move on later to 'What would you notice that is different which would indicate that you were closer to being the chairman you would like to be?' Alternatively, he might be asked to imagine a forthcoming board meeting at which he was going to be exactly the sort of chairman he wanted to be. Later he could be asked to identify how much of this 'ideal' description already occurs in his chairing role. Whatever the order, what is likely to make the difference is the degree of detail developed in the client's descriptions.

Preferred future questions

The aim of preferred future questioning is to help the client describe what difference the hoped-for outcome would make to their everyday life. Originally, this was a simple goal-setting exercise: the coach and client worked out how they would know it was time to say goodbye and indeed de Shazer and team at Milwaukee established a set of criteria for what they called 'well-formed goals' (de Shazer, 1991: 112). The goals they believed should be stated in positive, concrete and observable, detailed, small-step form and should be salient to the client. At this point goals were like targets: specific achievements that would mark the reaching of the journey's end. The coach and, to a lesser extent the client, would then devise strategies aimed at moving the client forward. This process is described in much of de Shazer's earlier work, for example in *Keys to Solution in Brief Therapy* (1985), when the influence of Milton Erickson was still very strong and de Shazer's team developed a whole series of indirect tasks designed to encourage the client to change. Although the shift from problem to solution was revolutionary the second revolution was still to come. Until then the coach would be very instrumental in the change process, gathering information about the client's successful past and possible future and then prescribing tasks to be performed between sessions in order to bring that future into the present. The thinking behind these tasks can be traced through de Shazer's first three books (de Shazer, 1983, 1985, 1988) and it is no surprise that many solution focused coaches have stayed with this early version of the approach. The more obviously instrumental the coach, and the more he or she can draw on knowledge not always available to the client, the more the client is likely to frame the coach as central to the change process.

Originally, the purpose of future focused questions was to clarify goals in order for coach and client to know when to stop. It was seen as an information-gathering process rather than one with the capacity to create new possibilities. The creative process was seen to be through the exploration of past and present solution-finding experiences (as will be seen in the section on *exceptions* in the next chapter) and the prescribing of tasks.

As is often the case, what was expected and what actually happened were not always the same. Firstly, clients who did not perform their allotted tasks were just as likely to report improvements as those who had completed everything asked of them. This finding meant that the significance of tasks was brought into question. Secondly, clients would often report significant improvements yet never achieve their specified 'goals'. This brought into question the link between goals and outcome. It was at this point that BRIEF began to define its unique brand of solution focused coaching: a brand not defined by a fixed set of techniques but by a rigorous discipline of questioning. Again, following in de Shazer's footsteps, Ockham's Razor, the principle of dynamic minimalism, became BRIEF's hallmark. This requires a constant re-examination of all aspects of practice and where possible matching beliefs to research: we should base what we do on the facts, what happens during and after coaching, rather than on the theory, what we imagine happens during and after coaching. The theory suggested that goals and tasks were central to solution focused coaching; the facts did not fit so BRIEF chose to follow the facts.

If the facts were suggesting some other change mechanism separate from tasks and that good outcomes did not require specific goals to be reached something else had to be going on. What this turned out to be was crystallised by a 17-year-old young man who at the end of a session asked 'Are you asking all these questions in order to assess me and advise me what to do or is it just the process of question and answer that's behind it?' An astonishing question! The coach answered: 'We used to think it was the assessment and advice but now we are beginning to think it might be just the conversation'. 'I agree entirely!' was the young man's response. He has gone on to great success in public life. Meanwhile, we began to look more closely at our practice.

The miracle question

The start of our search was the miracle question (de Shazer, 1988), an invention of the original Milwaukee team, which has become almost a trademark of solution focused coaching and is one of the most useful and creative starts to the process of eliciting a description of the preferred future.

Imagine that tonight, while you are asleep, a miracle happens and your best hopes from coming here are realised – but because you are asleep you can't know about this miracle. When you wake up tomorrow what are you going to notice different about your life that begins to tell you that this miracle has happened?

The miracle question therefore has four parts:

1 a miracle happens;
2 the miracle realises the wished-for outcome;
3 the client is asleep so can't know;
4 the future is to be 'discovered' – step by step.

The key part to this question and what rescues it from potentially unrealistic fantasy is the connection between the miracle and the contract: the miracle must always be the realisation of the hoped-for outcome, something not always appreciated in the early days of the solution focused approach. Unless this connection is made the question comes adrift from the purpose of the work and a less than helpful answer may well result. The value of the miracle metaphor is that it invites the client to use his or her imaginative creativity and this can be especially useful when the outcome seems near impossible or the client feels overwhelmed by a sense of hopelessness. Removing from the client any sense that he has to do anything himself to bring about the preferred state of affairs allows clients to imagine in a way that is not burdened and limited by their sense of the need to take action.

Although at first sight answers to the miracle question might be seen as 'goals' they were more often less definable. The client is asked for such mundane detail (e.g. 'What might you notice about yourself in the lift that showed you that you were feeling confident about the meeting ahead?') that most of the client's response would be too trivial to define as a 'goal'. The description would also be all-embracing and likely to include multiple perspectives of actions quite peripheral to what would be regarded as a goal (e.g. 'What might your partner notice about you when you returned home?'). A meticulous follow up of the miracle question did not so much lead to a description of goals but rather elicit a description of an entire future, a future that fitted with the client's hopes. We began to think of this as a 'preferred future' or the future that the client would like to head towards rather than an impending, less successful possibility.

The essential difference between a preferred future and a goal, or set of goals, is that the former is multifaceted and describes more a way of living than an arrival at a specific end. In some cases a preferred future might barely address the client's goal in a specific way. The following example is drawn from many conversations in which 'sleep' has been identified (usually mid-session) as a goal.

Client: And on top of everything else I sleep really badly!
Coach: So it would suit you to sleep better?
Client: It certainly would! But I'm not expecting miracles!
Coach: What difference would it make?
Client: A massive difference!
Coach: OK. Imagine you wake up tomorrow and the miracle you are not expecting has happened, you have begun sleeping as you would like to, what is the first thing you'll notice?
Client: I'd wake up refreshed.
Coach: And what difference would that make?
Client: I'd feel I could just get on with things.
Coach: What would be the first sign to you that the feeling was being translated into action?
Client: I'd get straight out of bed!
Coach: And then?
Client: I'd make the tea – instead of waiting for my partner to do it.
Coach: How else would your partner know you were getting on with things?

The session continues with a detailed description of a day of 'getting on with things' seen through the client's eyes and through the eyes of the many other witnesses to his day. In the latter part of the session attention is paid to how much of what is described is already happening. No further mention is made of sleep nor of the lethargy, lack of purpose or 'fogginess' that brought the client to coaching in the first place. And the client is very satisfied with the outcome; which includes a better sleeping pattern, more energy and a greater sense of purpose.

By avoiding goal setting we also leave the future with more fluidity. The client describes a possible future but does not need to commit to any part of it. One of the difficulties with goals, and even more so with plans to achieve them is that what seems logical and obvious today might prove foolish tomorrow. The 'preferred future' description allows for a myriad of differences which together create the idea that something different and better is perfectly possible without committing the client to any particular one of them. The client can begin the next day not so much with a path laid out but with a sense that what had seemed like an impenetrable jungle is now more of a pleasant wood. But the path through is left to the client.

Although the miracle question is a 'trademark' of solution focused coaching it is by no means the only way to start a conversation about the future. There is a strong argument for dispensing with the notion of a miracle except perhaps in very stuck or hopeless situations. As brief coaches have developed their practice over the years they have come to associate the speed of change with the invisibility of the coach. The more aware the client is of their own part in change the more likely they are to recognise their own success. The more visible the coach the more likely is the client to attribute success to the coach, which in turn may have the long-term effect of diminishing the client's confidence in their own powers. These are tentative hypotheses but ones that fit with Ockham's principle; put bluntly, do as little as possible!

Other preferred future entry-point questions

There are any number of possible doorways into a description of a potential and better future. Some of the more general openings might be as follows.

- 'If you woke up tomorrow and your "best hopes" had been realised what's the first thing you might notice different?'
- 'How will you know that things are improving?'

- 'How will you know that the problem is solved and you are moving into a more fitting future?'
- 'Let's imagine that tomorrow turns out to be a good day for you. How will you know that it is going well?'
- 'Suppose that you woke up this morning and just knew that you have achieved all that you wanted from coming here. What will you have noticed different in your life?'
- 'How will we know when it's time to stop meeting like this?'

Any questions that lead the client to describe something they want (or describe what would replace what they don't want) are preferred future questions. Whether the miracle question, or any other question, is used is of no importance; what is important is that the client is successfully invited to describe some aspect of a preferred future since being able to do so is associated with good outcomes in brief coaching.

In some situations it might be more pertinent to start the description at the workplace asking for example:

- 'What would be the first thing you'd notice as you walk through the door into work that would tell you that your confidence was growing in a way that was good for you and good for your team?'

Or at a more general level:

- 'What are some of the differences you would begin to notice at work if coming here proved useful?'

Different examples and why the coach might choose one question rather than another will be explored later.

Shifting from a negative to a positive outcome

Sometimes a client will respond to a preferred future question with a negative outcome, usually the absence of a problem or the cessation of a behaviour: the reduction of anxiety perhaps or the stopping of unfair treatment, maybe the client *not* dreading going to work or *not* having panic attacks. These initial responses are especially common if the client feels weighed down by the problem and cannot see a way out. The problem with these negative outcome statements is that although they might be of use in a problem-solving model where the focus is on reducing the frequency or severity of the problem's manifestations, they are of little use in a solution focused approach where the coach concentrates on building the preferred future – what will be happening when the problem is not. They give the coach no idea of what direction the client wants to take and therefore no way of knowing how to proceed.

It is crucial, therefore, to follow such answers with supplementary questions such as the following.

- 'What would you be doing instead (of feeling anxious)?'
- 'What do you hope will replace the unfair treatment?'
- 'If you didn't dread going into work what do you hope will take the place of that sense of dread?'
- 'What difference would it make if your panic attacks stopped?'

By asking the client what she will be doing *instead* of the problem or when the problem is solved, coach and client begin to get a sense of direction along which to build the conversation. This will occur over and over throughout the work; the client will answer a question with an 'absence', 'He won't be looking over my shoulder all the time', which is turned into a 'presence', a hoped-for outcome by the next question, or sometimes by a series of questions.

Coach: What would he be doing instead of looking over your shoulder?

Client: Just getting on with his own thing and trusting me to get on with mine.

Coach: And how would you know he was doing that, because he was trusting you more?

Client: Because he wouldn't be picking holes in everything I did.

Coach: What would he be doing instead?

Client: He might begin to appreciate what I do.

Coach: OK. So if your colleague began to appreciate you more would that be another sign that things were moving in the right direction?

However obvious the response to these questions might seem to be, the statement of positive outcomes is crucial if the client is to uncover the path they are seeking.

Moving from inner states to in-the-world action

Many clients begin their descriptions of their preferred futures in terms of internal states, descriptions of how they will be feeling differently when life is going better for them. Now just as the solution focused approach is not problem-phobic, neither is it feeling-phobic and yet constructing the preferred future in terms of internal feeling states can potentially slow the change process. Not only is it not possible for the coach to know what the client means by any feeling-state description, more importantly it may be hard for the client himself to notice that change is happening, particularly to notice the smallest of improvements or developments. For most of us noticing that we are just a little more relaxed, that we are a smidgeon more confident, that our patience with an irritating colleague has grown by a trifling amount is just difficult. However, when we describe these internal changes in terms of the outward evidence, what we will potentially be doing that fits with the internal change, the change itself can become more visible and in the process of the translation each sign that the client describes also represents a possible action step, each of which can represent a clue as to the way forward. So the solution focused coach will invite the client into the translation process with questions such as:

- 'So you will be more assertive – how will you know that you are more assertive?'
- 'What will you be doing that will tell others that your capacity to be assertive is growing?'
- 'Who will be the first person to notice the difference?'
- 'How will you notice others responding differently to you when you are being assertive in a way that is good for you and good for your whole team?'

This translation of inner states to outer actions is a key skill in the solution focused repertoire. This is not to say that 'inner states', including emotions, are not important, indeed they are a central part of our everyday existence. However, they have no currency in the world unless they are expressed in some way. Steve de Shazer liked to point out that this idea fits with Wittgenstein's thinking when he wrote 'every inner process stands in need of outward criteria' (cited in de Shazer 1991: 74). Since we live in a social world our very existence as human beings requires social interaction much of which takes place at a less than conscious level through body language, tone of voice, facial expression and the like. Although we can never know another person's inner state we can make educated guesses and respond accordingly. The more we recognise our own external manifestations of inner states, particularly those inner states we are seeking, the more able we are to recognise and even generate them.

This is especially important given the unreliability of inner states: waking up 'full of the joys of spring' is an inner state, as is waking up and not wanting to get out of bed. If we allowed these feelings to govern our actions our lives would be much curtailed. Instead, we learn from the days when we feel great the actions that get us through the others. On the days we don't feel so good we do what we have learned in order to get by. It is very common for people to experience crises of confidence at work and when these happen at key moments they can have disastrous effects such as the loss of a promotion possibility, failure to carry a creative idea forward or the inadequate handling of a staff member's incompetence. At such times, knowing what confidence would look like can help the client perform confidence without necessarily feeling it. Hence questions like: 'If you were feeling your confidence as you walked through the boardroom door what would be the first thing your Finance Director would notice?'

The more we can help our clients describe the actions, and the smaller the actions the better, the more they are likely to do them whether or not they are experiencing the associated emotion or inner state.

Moving from the general to the specific

Even some action-oriented descriptions benefit from a more detailed analysis. One of the commonest aspects of a manager's preferred future is to 'listen more'. This is certainly an action but one open to many different performances.

Coach: Who would be the first to notice that you were listening more?

Client: My PA [personal assistant], Karen, she'd definitely notice.

Coach: How would she know?

Client: I'd ask her more questions.

Coach: Like?

Client: Just chit-chat – how's her family and things like that.

Coach: Would she appreciate that?

Client: Yes, definitely!

Coach: How would you know?

Client: I think she'd be more relaxed.

Coach: And what difference would that make?

Client: She'd talk more – she has good ideas but I tend to be a bit impatient so I think she keeps a lot to herself now.

Coach: So if she talked more?

Client: We'd probably get things done a bit more efficiently, to be honest!

An entirely different form of 'listening more' might occur with a different colleague.

Coach: How would Harry know you were listening more?

Client: He'll notice that when he came in to ask me something I wouldn't be so impatient.

Coach: So what would you be instead?

Client: Patient!

Coach: And how would he know?

Client: I wouldn't stay on the computer as he was talking.

Coach: What would you do instead?

Client: I'd turn away from it and give him my full attention.

Coach: How would he know you were giving him your full attention?

Client: I'd look at him and maybe ask him to sit down.

For someone who does not see themselves as a good listener yet is being encouraged to be so by a more sensitive management culture, becoming a good listener might seem like a personality change: a major project! Translating this into specific face-to-face actions makes it not only a manageable change but a change based on the client's existing repertoire of possibilities since the descriptions can only have come from the client's experience of what is possible.

Building a detailed description

Describing the preferred future in as much detail as possible has two main benefits. It makes future change more noticeable since the client has now specified more potential indicators that they are moving in the right direction. When the client who wanted to be more confident in the boardroom describes a future where this confidence is present it will be made up of numerous small components many of which will exist outside the boardroom itself. Among other things these might include the way the client said goodbye to his children in the morning, the way he stood on the platform waiting for a train, the way he acknowledged another familiar passenger and the way he greeted the man on the security desk as he entered his office. In a busy life these inconsequential signs can go unnoticed especially when the focus is on the opposite signs: the signs of self-doubt and insecurity. What we notice has a significant effect on both our inner states and our outer actions so the more we are able to notice ourselves doing what we want to be doing the more of it we are likely to generate.

The second important aspect of detail is that it breaks big steps into smaller steps. 'I'll just have to control my drinking' might be a client's view of what they need to do in order to keep their job but if their drinking is out of control that is just what they won't be able to do. 'What might be the first thing you would notice on the day you began to control your drinking?' would be the beginning of a conversation aimed at charting a virtual (but possible) pathway to continued employment. We can set clients up to fail if we rely on only one or two indicators of progress, especially if these indicators are more than 'bite-sized'. The coach's ability to persist in teasing out small seemingly inconsequential details, sometimes with a relentlessness that challenges all social convention, is one of the keys to success with what many might be tempted to see as intractable problems. Helping clients move beyond the more obvious answers, 'headline' answers into the 'small print' of their future story is at the very heart of solution focused coaching.

Other person perspective questions

How we are viewed by others is as important in the workplace as it is in life as instruments such as 360 degree appraisals testify. Less obvious is the importance of our perceptions of how we are viewed. Although 'strong' people are said to be people who do not mind what other people think of them, their strength will come from experiencing respect and acceptance from enough significant people to engender the confidence they have to 'be themselves'. How we imagine we are perceived by others makes up a significant part of our sense of self. How could it not if our very survival depends on sociability: the capacity to collaborate with others towards common ends. In exploring the details of our clients' lives, past, present and future, solution focused coaches pay great attention to their clients' views of themselves through the eyes of others. These others may be significant or not. They are, in the first instance, simply alternative viewpoints through which the client is able to widen his or her self-description. At the least significant end our client wanting to be more confident in the boardroom might be asked a question like:

- 'How would other passengers on the train up to town know that you were feeling confident?'

This invites the client to recognise some of the actions, for example shoulders relaxed, head up, eye contact, smooth brow, that signify confidence. The immediate context might not in itself be significant but if the journey being taken is to culminate in an important meeting and a favourable decision then each and every aspect of confidence will have a potential part to play. A more significant 'witness' might have been 'called' prior to the train journey:

- 'How will your wife know you are leaving the house feeling your confidence?'

This is calling on a more significant 'witness' and one more likely to have a finer-tuned description. Even more significant in this context might be the view of the panel:

- 'What is the first thing your deputy will notice about you as you enter the boardroom that tells him you are entering with all your confidence at hand?'
- 'In those last few seconds before you begin to present your plan what will tell you that you are about to speak with confidence?'

If 20 minutes have been spent detailing all the confident behaviour prior to this moment, if the client has experienced each answer as within not just the realms of possibility but also within his existing repertoire of behaviours, the description of confident behaviour in the boardroom is likely to flow with the same ease as the less consequential descriptions; the boardroom performance will be just one more expression of this overall confidence, which by then will seem almost inevitable.

If the client's view of themselves is like a two-dimensional photograph then the multi-perspectival view might be seen as a sculpture: something to take a walk around. A richness is provided as well as a concrete recognition of the social environment in which we all live our lives.

Developing an interactional view

Of all the many levels of description that occur within a solution focused conversation, the views of self and others in relation to feelings, thoughts, actions and words, undoubtedly the most powerful are descriptions of interactions. It is these descriptions that help engender the changes in others necessary to support the client's endeavours to move forward. The notion that a conversation between coach and client might change the behaviour of a third person totally incognisant of the conversation might at first seem far-fetched.

However, we have these conversations all the time: parents talk about their children, workers talk about their bosses, salesmen talk about their customers. These are all conversations that include the purpose of influencing third parties to fit in with our hopes and plans.

The difference with solution focused conversations is that the 'chain of influence' is indirect. And possibly more powerful. Other person perspective questions are expanded to include interactional behaviour with sequences such as:

- 'Who, other than you, will be the first person to notice that you're doing something different?'
- 'What will s/he see that is different?'
- 'Who else will notice? What will s/he see?'
- 'How might he/she respond?'
- 'And if they did that, how would you respond to them?'
- 'How would your relationship be then?'

In the following example a senior partner is feeling undervalued by his peer with whom he had set up the business many years before. The client is finding the situation so difficult he is considering early retirement but is afraid his partner will try to secure an unfair deal. On balance he would prefer to stay but cannot envisage this unless his partner changes.

Coach: So let's imagine that he does change and it happens tonight; what's the first thing you'll notice tomorrow that tells you he has changed and become more like his old self?

Client: The first thing I'd notice is that I wasn't dreading going in.

Coach: How would you be instead?

Client: I'd be looking forward to it. We've got some very interesting stuff going on at the moment, some of it right up my street, and if I knew he wasn't going to be looking over my shoulder like he's been doing, or even taking my files when I'm not in and then sending nasty emails and criticising me in front of junior staff – you can see how difficult this has become and why I'm at my wits' end *(more description of the recent history which the coach listens to but does not explore).*

Coach: What difference would it make to the start of your day if you found yourself approaching the office with a sense of looking forward?

Client: Oh! A huge difference!

Coach: What would be the first difference?

Client: I wouldn't be creeping in for one thing.

Coach: What would you do instead?

Client: I'd probably go into the main office, see who's in and say hello. There's usually one or two early birds but recently I've avoided going in there unless I absolutely have to. He's quite likely to have a go at me even in front of the office team. I find it so humiliating. I suppose I should stand up to him but when I do it makes him even worse. I've tried to explain how I feel and to ask him what he wants from me but each time he says he's too busy and next thing I'm getting even more critical emails.

Coach: Who would be the first to notice that you were looking forward to the day?

Client: My PA. She'd definitely notice.

Coach: What would she see?

Client: I'd say hello, be more cheerful, ask about her family – all the things I used to do before all this began to happen. I know she's finding it difficult and is even thinking of leaving.

Coach: And how would she respond?

Client: She'd be delighted!

Coach: How would you know?

Client: She'd say! I know she worries about me. No, she'd say something like 'You're in a good mood today!' Maybe make a joke.

Coach: And how would you respond?

Client: I'd probably make a joke back and we'd get on and plan the day.

Coach: Would she be pleased?

Client: Absolutely, I can't remember when we last sat down at the beginning of the day. I think she's been avoiding me as much as I've been avoiding her, especially since he's been giving her work which he shouldn't because he's got his own PA but she's not as good as mine. That's part of the problem!

Coach: How would you know she was pleased?

Client: She'd be enthusiastic and want to get on with the day's work.

Coach: And what would she notice about you?

Client: I'd have my old confidence back and more to the point I'd be able to concentrate again. That would be the big difference – I'd be able to concentrate on the job in hand instead of worrying about the next broadside from him.

Coach: And what difference would that make?

Client: More work would get done. I suppose I'd feel I was pulling my weight again because to be honest with all this going on my work has definitely suffered so I can see his point sometimes even though I think it's him that's brought it all on.

The chain of influence is easily traceable. Given an imaginary starting point in which the desired outcome has been achieved the client describes first his behaviour, then his behaviour through the eyes of others and then moves on to a description of interaction: the effect he has on others and they on him. The difference between the descriptions invited by the coach and those volunteered by the client is that the former describe virtuous cycles and the latter their opposite. One leads to a sense of possibility whereas the other leads to limitation and closure. As the description continues further into the day the impact of the client on others becomes increasingly obvious and within a few minutes he is able to envisage the beginning of a very different relationship with his partner.

Coach: When would you first see your partner?

Client: I know he took one of my files last night and I was expecting trouble today – for some reason he's been quiet. But I fully expect him to barge into my room any time with the file.

Coach: So if he does that while you are with your PA what's the first thing he'll notice about you?

Client: You know, I think I'd just tell him to wait. Tell him I'm busy and will come over to his office when I've finished.

Coach: And how do you think he'll respond?

Client: He'll be shocked! Stunned probably – and then he'd leave.

When seeking descriptions of these interactions it is helpful to distinguish between the wished-for and the most likely responses of significant others. The client might *wish* that their partner said something considerate in response to a new behaviour but might think that he is more *likely* to say something disparaging. In such instances the clients can be asked to describe their response to the disparagement within the frame of their preferred future. In the above example the description begins with an unlikely starting point, the transformation of the 'offending' partner. However, once the client is established in what his side of this very different equation would look like, the scenario returns to a more likely version of the partner's behaviour. At this point the client is ready to consider a change in his own behaviour which will inevitably lead to a change in his partner's.

Once the description of change has begun further problem areas can be reviewed in this new light.

- 'So what would you notice different about your response if you were feeling all the confidence you wanted and he tried to put you down?'
- 'How would you respond to being blamed for something you didn't do in a way that was right for you and yet not feel forced to take early retirement?'
- 'And when you responded like that how do you think your colleague would respond?'

In this way clients are helped to chart their own way through some of the difficult situations that have hitherto tripped them up. A key idea here is that whatever the client does it needs to be 'right' for them while at the same time not leading them into consequences that could cause more trouble. The fit with the client's context is routinely held central through the process of questioning.

Preferred futures, goals, targets and tasks

Many solution focused coaches will encourage clients to talk about and to set goals and, as we have seen, early solution focused practitioners did, indeed, think and work this way. This can work very well when the client has specific and discrete and easily planned goals such as completing a project on time. Most clients, however, want more than simple work management targets. Typical outcome requests are greater assertiveness, a better working relationship with a particular colleague, team leadership skills, a reduction in anxiety and stress, a better work–life balance, more creativity or more productivity. Mapping out a 'small print' description of a future where this outcome has been achieved is not the precursor to specific plans, targets and tasks. In most cases the client's answers will be a sufficient intervention to inspire movement towards a better future. This is one of the harder lessons for many coaches to learn. Trusting the client to listen and respond to their own words frees the coach from the temptation to overinvest in the client's future. When the coach sees the task as *getting* the client to do something different the client is likely to experience an overinvolvement that impedes rather than encourages progress. Brian Cade recently reminded us of one of his 'important rules' (Cade, 2009: 116) that 'It is important never to be more enthusiastic about the need for any particular change than is the client,' since when this happens the client is only left with the arguments for no change!

The plans and targets generated in a typical goal-setting conversation can themselves become an impediment to progress. They can only be based on a prediction of what the future holds and as this can only be guessed at we can only guess at the right plans and targets. This becomes apparent at second and subsequent coaching sessions where the client has moved forward but in a different direction to the imagined future described in the previous session. One client, for example, described a possible future that would lead to a move to a better and more interesting job. Part of the imagined route was to improve her performance in her current position in order to provide a solid platform for change. By the second session a month later she was enjoying her job so much that not only had she decided to stay but unexpected possibilities of advancement had become apparent.

Any plans and targets aimed at changing jobs might well have interfered with such a good outcome. Instead the coach had let the description do its work, which many clients have described as opening up a sense of possibility. Mostly when we find ourselves stuck in a certain aspect of our lives it is because we have lost a sense of possibility. We know we don't like where we are but we cannot see a possibility of being somewhere else; if we could we would be striving towards it. When a client describes in rich concrete detail what a hoped-for future might look like one aim is to create a virtual experience that engenders the possibility of being somewhere else. This in turn awakens the client's creativity: once an alternative to the stuck state seems possible most of us will set off in that direction. Once we are moving again the world looks different; we can see more and so more choices become apparent and imagined pathways will sometimes turn out to be less tempting.

Summary

- Solution focused coaches ask their clients questions that enable the client to describe, in detail, how life will be when they have achieved their 'best hopes' for the coaching process.
- The approach has designed a range of questions that seem effective in supporting clients in developing their descriptions.
- Solution focused coaches invite their clients to describe their preferred future possibilities in positive rather than negative terms, and to describe these states in terms of in-the-world actions rather than inner states.
- Building these pictures in detail seems to be associated with a greater likelihood of change and one of the tools that the solution focused coach will use to achieve this progress is to ask 'other person perspective questions'.
- Do not be dominated by plan and target setting; trusting the client to listen to his own words and make his own decisions will be just as effective and a lot more economical.

Activity: Developing yourself

- Picture a quality that you yourself might like to have more of in your working life.
- Imagine that on your next day at work you do have more of this quality.
- List ten differences, however small, that you will notice about yourself when you bring more of this quality to work.
- List ten differences that those with whom you interact at work, clients, colleagues, boss, others, will notice about you.
- When they notice those differences how might they respond differently to you? (seven differences)
- And how might you respond differently to them? (seven differences)
- And imagine that this change happens slowly over time – what might be the first and tiniest changes that you might notice?

5

What is already working?

Once the client has described his preferred future, the next stage of the work is to look at what is already working and what has worked in the past. One of the key starting points of solution focused thinking was the notion of *exceptions*: the idea that however bad a problem is, there will always be times when it is worse, and therefore inevitably there must also be times when it is not so bad or even totally absent. This means that all clients must of necessity already be doing something that can be seen as useful in constructing the future that they are hoping to move towards. Very often the client will not have noticed these moments, these ante-cedents of possibility. Interestingly, it was a very similar idea to this that independently inspired appreciative inquiry (Cooperrider and Whitney, 1999) although the ways that the two models have developed is substantially different.

Finding out what is already working can take many forms and sometimes it will be the main focus of the work. A client will sometimes respond to being asked their 'best hopes' from the coaching with a vague sense of uncertainty about whether or not they are doing a good enough job. This could be a client at any level from senior board member to most junior manager. To ask such a client what they would be doing differently if they were 'good enough' immediately implies shortcomings that might not be justified. In such situations the coach might best begin by asking the client to specify what they think they are doing well. Aiming at a list of fifty or even one hundred things they do well will usually have a two-fold effect. Firstly, the client is likely to have reassured himself that in many ways he is doing a good job already; and, secondly, this reassurance is likely to awaken him to even more possibilities. Any improvement in performance will have arisen entirely out of this increased self-confidence and will therefore be much more likely to last.

Pre-meeting change

By the time of the first appointment it is not at all unusual for the client already to have made constructive changes in her life. This should not surprise us since the change process, for the client, will start way before she arrives for the first appointment. This fact is often obscured by our own professional-centric view of the change process. Since we can fall in to the trap of seeing ourselves as the main change agents, then we can tend to assume that significant change will only start when the client walks into our office. This limiting assumption holds the risk of making the changes that clients have already made harder to see. In fact of course the process of change will actually have started at the point that the client first thought of talking with someone, and is already well established at the point of the client making an appointment. The making of an appointment is in itself likely to hold new meanings for the client, which will in their turn make a difference, so more change is likely while the client waits for the appointment to come. Once the client arrives with us therefore the client is well into change, their relationship with the issue that has been bothering them has already inevitably shifted substantially and it is entirely reasonable to assume that that internal change will be reflected in changes visible in the client's world. Therefore when the coach meets the client it is expectable that the majority of clients will already have begun taking steps towards a solution themselves and if what they have done can be identified during the first session it serves to emphasise their motivation, skills and possibilities. This effect can be strengthened if at the time of scheduling the first appointment the coach invites the client to look out for any signs of positive change. The coach will then begin the first session by asking about pre-treatment change (Weiner-Davis et al., 1987). Change achieved before the formal beginning of coaching is likely to be particularly valued by the client since she will tend to 'own' it fully. Steve de Shazer writes in *Clues* (1988: 5) 'From the beginning of the first session the therapist and the client are constructing a therapeutic reality based on *continuing* transformation or change rather than on *initiating* change'.

Having asked the client to look out for changes the coach might ask:

- 'So, what changes have you noticed since you rang to make the appointment?'
- 'What do you think you did to set off this process?'
- 'What difference is that change making?'
- 'If instead of making that change before we met it had happened after our first session what would you think of the value of coaching?'

If the client reports no changes the coach can just be non-committal and get on with the work probably by asking:

- 'So what are your best hopes from our meeting today?'
- 'So if this meeting turns out to be useful where do you hope it will lead you?'
- 'Let's begin by working out how we'll know when it's time to stop meeting like this!'

Exceptions

In the earliest days of solution focused brief therapy, the emphasis was on identifying times the problem happened less or not at all. There was minimal emphasis on the future, which tended to be described in broad brush strokes. The times the problem happened less were called exceptions (de Shazer, 1985), to emphasise the exceptional times that would often be missed by clients and others. By asking questions that drew the client's attention to these happenings, the client could consider what they did and how they did it. At the start of a session conducted in 1990 by Steve de Shazer with a client of one of the BRIEF team, the client began by describing the problem:

Client: It's money problems, I spend a lot of money, sneak it out, our rent, food money . . .

de Shazer: When was the last time you resisted the urge to spend the money?

Client: *(pauses, taken by surprise)* Well, I must admit it's been this week.

de Shazer: This week. Today, yesterday?

Client: Today!

de Shazer: How did you do it?

A significant part of the session was then spent on helping the client remember all the times when he controlled his urge to spend money. There were so many that he could no longer define himself as being out of control and for the first time he began to see a future where this would no longer be a problem.

In a more recent case a client half jokingly raised a problem as he was about to leave. Throughout the meeting he had displayed a slight facial tic, which he did not mention and neither did the coach. If the client elects to not raise an issue it would be unusual for the coach to see it as her business. This did not stop the coach quietly admiring the man for getting on with his very public life despite the slightly unnerving tic.

Client: *(Pointing to his eye)* Don't suppose you can do anything about this?

Coach: We could certainly talk about it next time. How do you control it at the moment?

Client: I don't. I've had it since my teens – I suppose I always will.

Coach: What about when you need to control it – when it would really get in the way?

Client: Sometimes I count to ten and make myself relax, especially if I'm meeting someone for the first time and need to make a good impression. It doesn't always work though.

Coach: What else do you do when you really need to?

Client: Breathing can help. Sometimes I can sense it coming on and if I can take a few deep breaths it helps.

Coach: OK, that's two ways already and if we had time I imagine we'd find some more. If you look out for them over the next few weeks it will give us a good start next time.

A month later the client reported that the tics had stopped after the last session.

It was the realisation that nobody is perfect and nobody can do their problems perfectly either that led to the idea of exceptions and the beginning of the solution focused approach. The fact that whatever the problem there will always be exceptions means that however entrenched and stuck a client is they will always be 'doing' potential solutions or alternatives to the problem. Finding and amplifying these exceptions was the early route to solution and formed the basis of the approach. However, for a solution focused process that held that amplifying 'solution talk' is associated with a greater chance of solutions developing, this exception route was clearly problematic since to find exceptions the coach needed to hear about the problem even though information about the problem itself was not necessary except to establish the exceptions to it. This logical 'problem' at the heart of early solution focus was solved by introducing a picturing of the desired outcome as the starting point to the process.

The advantage of asking about the preferred future first and *then* finding exceptions that arise from the description of that future is that the exceptions will relate specifically to what the client wants to happen in future. Starting with exceptions means that there is always a risk that what the client describes is likely to relate more to the problem than what they want in future.

Client: I'm not drinking so much.
Coach: What have you been doing instead?
Client: Actually, I've been using more drugs!

This may indeed be an exception to the problem, but hardly one that the coach can encourage even though in the short term taking drugs might be less obvious at work than being drunk.

Once the preferred future is clarified, both in the first session and later ones, exception questions can be more aligned to the hoped-for outcome.

- 'Tell me about the times that you are not (or less) stressed?'
- 'What about the weeks when that feeling of being out of control comes to you less often?'
- 'I guess that there are times that you resist the urge to be overcritical – how do you do that?'
- 'What about times when you refuse to allow your habit to control you and your life?'
- 'When was the last time that you said "no" to that particular temptation?'

Some exceptions can seem very small at first:

- 'What about those days when that feeling of misery at work is just a little less overpowering? What is it that is different on those days?'

Exception questions are especially useful when the client is very problem focused and is wanting to stay close to the problem in his talking. Exception questions offer the coach a pathway into solution-talk that feels to the client significantly problem related so that the shift of focus that the client is required to make is fairly small and thus often represents an easier fit to the client's talking. Exception questions can also be of particular use when the client takes the view that the problem is substantially beyond his control. Discovering those times when the problem could have happened and did not inevitably leads the client to begin to question their framing and that is amplified when the coach begins to enquire 'so how did you do that?' In a similar way exception questions can be useful in inviting clients to begin to question their own fixed views of others, deconstructing the client's *always* and *never* descriptions of the problem pattern.

- 'What's different about the times he is not irritating you?'
- 'When do you feel least criticised by your team?'
- 'What about when she does not just ignore your ideas?'

Mostly, however, the solution focused coach will be less interested in when the problem doesn't happen and more interested in when the preferred future is happening already.

Instances: Signs of the preferred future already happening

While clients are describing what will be different when their best hopes are achieved, from time to time they spontaneously refer to instances of that future *already* happening. For example, while describing how a better relationship with a colleague would look tomorrow, they might suddenly add, 'a bit like it was yesterday'.

- 'So, what else would be different tomorrow if things were a bit more like they were yesterday?'
- 'What was different about yesterday – what did you do?'
- 'When else have you noticed this difference?'
- 'What other parts of the future that you are looking to build are already happening?'
- 'What difference has this made to your hopes for the future?'

The solution focused coach's preference for working with instances rather than exceptions relates simply to the notion that when using the approach the coach is looking to invite the client to refocus, to focus more on the future and what she wants, rather than on the past, the problem and what is not wanted. Naturally in order for the client to think about exceptions, the client has to hold in mind the problem. In order to think about times when we do not get angry we have to hold the idea of the times when we do indeed get angry, which can feed the client's often self-limiting idea of herself as 'an angry person'. If on the other hand the client can be invited to specify that her best hopes for the coaching are to find ways of being in control, the client can then be invited to identify instances of in-control behaviour without the question requiring that she bring the 'angry person' to mind. Asking about instances allows the client to step further in to the world of solution. The more that we focus on anger, either its presence or its absence, the more risk there is that the client's problem-dominated idea of who she is will be supported, and that the change process will be slowed. As we know human brains are not very good at processing the word 'not'. When we say to ourselves 'I wish he were not so rude', what stays with us is the idea of the other as 'rude', just confirming and rigidifying our view.

However, there are times when to focus directly on instances involves the client in having to make too big a leap and the smaller shift into the world of exceptions can represent an easier staging-post, a transitional focus on the journey into solution-talk. Every question that we ask has to make sense in the context of the client's world view. If the question makes no sense then it will be challenged or rejected. So were a client who has been feeling overwhelmed by their situation to be asked, for example, 'so what has been brilliant for you at work over the past month?', the question, being too far from their experience will make no sense, will not fit and is likely, one way or another, to be rejected. So for a client in the depths of despair a closer question is required, yet one that will still invite her into the world of possibilities. So in making a judgement the coach will always be looking for questions that fit well enough to make sense but which also hold within them the possibility of a shift in the client's focus. And the ideal question might be the one that represents the biggest step into solution-talk that the client can manage. So if to talk with the client about instances when the hoped-for future is already happening is a step too far, then it might make sense to the client to focus on exceptions, and if that is too great a leap then perhaps focusing on the client's coping might be more appropriate. Sometimes, as with the case of 'Maurice' below, even this is rebuffed. Mostly however, even the most despondent client will respond to 'coping' or 'stopping things getting worse' questions.

Getting by, coping and survival

Occasionally a client will present an issue which, at least for the time being, is not solvable and therefore the best that can be hoped for is that the client find a way of managing the situation, or coping, in the best possible way. Andrew was referred by the occupational health service of the education authority that employed him, having recently taking up a senior management post in a school for children with special educational needs. He very quickly realised that everyday working life in the school was far tougher and more challenging than he had appreciated and within a month of appointment he was feeling severely stressed, waking up each morning wishing that he could stay at home, indeed wishing that he could stay in bed. In the short term Andrew saw nothing that he could do to change his working environment. The head teacher he described as 'burnt out', many of the teaching team were short-term supply staff and the pupils' out-of-control and challenging behaviour was unlikely to be turned around in a mere matter of weeks. As Andrew described the nightmare situation in which he felt that he found himself the coach began to ask him about his best hopes for the work. After a lengthy period of talking Andrew concluded that all that he could reasonably hope for was to find a way of surviving the situation intact – initially with the idea of getting through to the end of the first term and then resigning. Focusing on his survival made sense to Andrew and very quickly coach and client were noting those days when Andrew felt that he had got through the trials and stresses of the day a little more easily. Andrew's professional commitment was reflected in him finding a way of staying at the school for 2 years and contributing in no small part to the recovery of the institution before moving on.

In the following example a client was overseeing a programme of redundancies within which, somewhat ironically, not only her team but she herself were to be 'let go'. As an human resources (HR) manager in an organisation that was constantly down-sizing (and up-sizing with consultants and temporarily contracted staff) she had coached many colleagues through the process. But this did not make it easier for her.

Client: You'd think it would be easier, but it isn't!
Coach: No! I guess it just has to be lived through. What are your ways of doing that?
Client: I'm not sure I am.
Coach: So how do you get yourself into work each day?
Client: With great difficulty.
Coach: How?
Client: I haven't got much choice, have I?

Coach: You could go off sick!
Client: I wouldn't do that! Well, I hope not though to be honest I'd have a good case.
Coach: So how come you stick with it?
Client: It's partly pride – I don't want to be beaten.
Coach: So how *do* you get through the day?
Client: I just try to immerse myself in the work – there's lots to do – organising your own sacking!
Coach: So pride, determination, refusal to be beaten, sense of humour and – what else keeps you hanging on in there?

Later, when the coach has elicited several more 'coping skills' it will be possible to begin creating a more hopeful prospect.

Coach: When this phase is over and you are getting on with whatever will be coming next, what will tell you that sticking with it, refusing to be beaten, had been the right thing for you, not only then but for your future?
Client: I think it would be my confidence.

It is very important that the coach does not try to change the client's mind when they are feeling stuck and hopeless. This will serve only to encourage the client to make a stronger case for their plight. Instead, the coach needs to acknowledge and accept the client's position but without actually accepting the limitations that the client is attaching. This is done not by challenging the client but by accepting and then *adding* to the client's view:

- 'How on earth, after a day like that, did you even manage to get up the next morning, let alone take yourself into work?'
- 'I would imagine a lot of people would have given up at that point – how come you didn't? How did you keep yourself going?'
- 'I don't think there are many things more stressful and undermining than being bullied – where did you find the courage to face it day after day?'
- 'As an HR person yourself, with all the knowledge about what's involved and what this can do to people, how would

you rate your performance if you were watching yourself from outside?'

One of the surest signs to the coach that he or she is losing touch with the client is when either coach or client is heard to say 'Yes, but . . .' This almost always means that the coach is not listening closely enough to what the client is saying but instead has become too invested in getting his or her own message across. As soon as we start 'yes butting' our client we are in effect arguing with their perception. The word *but* is an exclusive word, either this is right or that is right, both cannot be right. And clearly what we notice time and again is that in arguments most people tend to rigidify their positions, arguing more and more strongly for their own rightness. And the more we persist in our own perception the greater the risk that the client will rehearse over and over the reasons for their own competing view. The effect of this is normally merely to entrench the client in their own problem-dominated view. Luckily in this example the coach notices quickly his mistake.

Client: I've been so stressed for most of this year I'm beginning to think it's not worth it – I'd be better off packing it in!

Coach: Yes, but you've got the best sales record for the second year running!

Client: Yeah but at what a price!

Coach: *(Realising the mistake!)* Yes, I guess that's right and it's not always easy for someone in such a competitive world to even recognise let alone admit to stress.

Client: No. if people knew I'd come here they'd see it as weakness.

Coach: So how did you manage to overcome that pressure and take a step to look after yourself a bit more?

Client: I just knew I had to find a way to get more of a balance otherwise I was heading for some sort of breakdown.

Coaches, like their clients, are far from perfect and in any session are likely to make mistakes. In the above example the coach had become more invested in his client's wish to succeed than the client himself. However, once he realised this he was able to realign himself to the client, include a more fitting compliment and begin to work together towards a more positive agenda – a better work–life balance.

The solution focused approach, although often described by both clients and coaches as a very positive way of working is never in the business of denying, minimising or trivialising the issue that the client brings to the table. The solution focused coach will never try to persuade the client that things are not as bad as he says, or that really he is managing better than he feels. Faced with the coach's denial of the client's experience most clients will choose either to withdraw or to increase their efforts to demonstrate just how tough life is for them. Far easier for the coach just to accept the client's position and to build a platform of acceptance from which a solution focused question can fittingly be asked.

- 'It sounds as if things have been really tough for you over the past few weeks so, given that, given that things have been so difficult, what on earth have you been doing that has been helping you to get through at all?'

It is clear in this example that the coach is not attempting in any way to minimise the client's experience, the use of 'given that' tying together the tough time and the new focus, the client's coping through that tough time. Bill O'Hanlon (2001) has often said that coaches must always have one foot in acknowledgement and the other foot in possibility and that throughout every meeting the coach must flexibly shift her weight between these two positions, back and forth, this way and that, in order to ensure that the client always feels sufficiently heard in order to be able to engage but is not invited to linger in the world of problem a minute more than necessary. This ability is one of the key skills of the solution focused approach. Coaches who try to move their clients on before the client is able or ready risk becoming 'solution forced' (Nylund and Corsiglia, 1994) and losing their clients' cooperation, whereas those who believe that problems have to be ventilated, that they have to be got out in some conversational equivalent to a surgical intervention, risk slowing the change process down and potentially wasting the client's time.

Stopping things getting worse

Occasionally, clients are so overwhelmed by what they are going through that not only can they not see anything of value, they cannot see how they are coping. In these sessions the most mundane and routine aspects of a client's life can take on a significance not usually accorded them. How a client still gets up, goes into work on time, performs their routine duties and whatever else they are doing in what they perceive as untenable circumstances gives recognition to their struggle and values the many acts of 'keeping on going' that might at some point lead towards a better future. In these circumstances the coach might become curious about what is stopping things getting worse. When the work enters this zone, especially if redundancy and unemployment are issues facing the client, a coach must be prepared for anything including the client bringing up the possibility of suicide. Although coaches might not see such personal problems as within their legitimate remit they cannot shut up shop immediately they arise. They have a responsibility to deal, at least in the immediate term, with whatever arises in the session.

Client: I'm getting very close to thinking what's the point? Why not end it all?

Coach: OK, so difficult as it is to imagine, things could get even worse.

Client: Thanks for reminding me.

Coach: So what's stopping it getting even worse? What are you doing that is keeping you off the bottom?

Client: Being here, maybe.

Coach: And it wasn't an easy journey – what decided you to make the trip?

Client: To be honest I was going to cancel because I couldn't really see much of a point.

Coach: So how did you get yourself to come even though you couldn't see much of a point?

Client: I thought I'd give it a try. Nothing to lose!

Coach: What is it about you that even though you can't see much of a point you are still prepared to give something a try?

Client: Maybe it means I haven't totally given up hope.

Coach: So what has that hanging on to some vestige of hope got you to do, apart from coming here?

Client: Well I still get up in the morning, go through the motions, shop, eat. What else can I do?

Coach: So how come you haven't given up? What is it that gets you to go through the motions even when you are feeling so bad?

As the coach continues to glean information about the client's coping capacities and the actions through which these capacities are evidenced the possibility of more future focused questions begins to open up.

Coach: And if coming here, hanging on, getting up each day, going through the motions turns out to be worth it what will be the first sign to you that things are, at last, beginning to improve?

Client: I suppose I'd feel more like getting up in the mornings.

The pre-problem state

Occasionally, when all else fails, a client might be invited to talk about life before the problem. This is fraught with difficulties not least because that time might be so disconnected from the present or the circumstances might be so different that no useful comparison can be made. If a person has experienced a major life-changing event it is often difficult to refer back to previous achievements as a basis for current solutions, the discontinuity is too great: the way a person experienced happiness before depression is not likely to offer many clues about how to find happiness when in the depression's grip. That is, not without some joining conversation to bridge the gap as happened with Maurice, a respected head of a technical department of a large company.

Maurice was suffering from depression and had been on long-term sick leave for almost 6 months. His employer's occupational physician, who knew of BRIEF's work, referred him as a last resort before pursuing a more disciplinary route. It was the threat of dismissal that brought Maurice to coaching but he could see no good coming from it. When asked about his hopes he said that obviously he wanted to get back to work but saw no possibility of this happening; in fact, he saw no possibility of anything happening and it was only because he wasn't going to let his employer off the hook that he had not 'ended it all'. When the coach asked Maurice how he would know that he was beginning to move in the direction of going back to work he became angry and threatened to leave. 'There is no future, so don't ask questions about something that doesn't exist!' Changing tack the coach asked about exceptions, those times when Maurice felt that getting back to work was not entirely impossible. Maurice said he no longer had such times and again grew angry when pressed. When the coach can find no way into the future or into exceptions he will fall back to 'coping questions'.

Acknowledging the tremendous difficulties Maurice has had to handle both with his mental health and in his relationship with his employers the coach asked Maurice how he had managed to keep going. At first Maurice was interested in this question but quickly became irritated: 'It doesn't matter how I coped. What matters is that I'm not coping now!' Rebuffed once again the coach had few places to go. The last resort is compliments. For Maurice these might have included his straightforwardness, his willingness to look straight into the void and not pretend that there was something there, his ability to keep going however he managed to do it, his strong sense of justice and determination to fight his corner. The purpose would be for the coach to demonstrate the genuineness of his good intentions by the specificity and accuracy of the compliments. As will be seen later compliments have had a significant place in solution focused coaching and their continued significance is likely to be in their capacity to demonstrate good intentions. However, before this final attempt at engagement one more focus can be tried:

Coach: Maurice, how come the company is putting so much time and energy into you, even bringing us in?

Client: Because they want to get rid of me.

Coach: Maybe. On the other hand they aren't known for their generosity towards staff and I know they have got rid of people without bothering anything like as much as they are with you.

Client: Yes, well they know not to mess with me!

Coach: So they must have rated you when you were working to be going so carefully now?

Client: They used to before all this lot came in.

Coach: And I guess they had good reason – what sort of reputation did you have before all this started?

Client: I used to meet with the MD [Managing Director] most weeks even though I wasn't officially at that level. He reckoned they would probably have gone bust if it wasn't for me. That's how highly I was rated. But this lot –

Coach: OK. I'm beginning to get a glimpse of why you are so angry as well as a sense of what has kept you going through such a terrible time.

Client: It's not going to keep me going for much longer – I'm just about finished.

Coach: If it did? If it kept you going just long enough to turn the corner and begin to pay off, what would be the first sign? The first sign it had been worth it?

Client: They might start to bloody listen!

Coach: What difference might that make?

Client: I'm not asking for much – if they treated me with a bit more respect maybe I'd do the same back.

Coach: How would you know they were beginning to listen? What would be the first indication if they began to do that?

Client: One thing would be not to be treated like a minion. I've known the head of HR for over 10 years, we've even had the odd beer together and he wrote 'Dear Mr Smith'. Why not 'Dear Maurice?'

Coach: And if he did that?

Client: Then I'd be more inclined to go half way.

'Go half way' provides the starting point for the description of an alternative future. By keeping the description detailed and interactional the possibility of a more productive relationship between Maurice and his employers is traced. Although it has begun with a different sort of letter it is not dependent upon this. The description is so detailed and mundane many alternative starting points become obvious. The coach does not point this out, does not try to push Maurice in a particular direction but instead trusts that Maurice will make the best decision he can, bearing in mind that his initial stated hope was to get back to work. Which Maurice eventually did.

Referring on

At some point in a coaching session where the client has raised issues beyond the coach's remit consideration needs to be given to a referral on. This would be particularly important in the example above where the client has indicated the possibility of self-harm. This does not mean the coach must 'flee the scene'. Rather the opposite. As the only other person on the scene and as a person skilled in managing useful conversations the coach has a potentially significant part to play. Taking the client seriously, being curious about coping skills and future possibilities all have great potential for helping the client through a difficult chapter in their life. By asking the client to evaluate his or her safety or the need for a referral on to a more therapeutic service the coach continues to treat the client as an expert while positively recognising their vulnerability. The message the client will have received is that the coach has remained interested in them and also accepting of them in their entirety at the same time as being professional and honest enough to know and be open about his or her limitations.

Different coaches will have different guidelines about when to refer on (and some will have none). A solution focused coach would seek the client's view about the necessity of a referral or at least the passing on of information.

Coach: Earlier on you mentioned the possibility of ending it all – is that something I need to be concerned about?

Client: How do you mean?

Coach: Well, if it was a serious possibility I would preferably like you to see someone more knowledgeable than me in that field, someone who could offer you more help but I would also have to pass on my worries to your GP [general practitioner] because we all have a responsibility to look after each other's safety.

Client: Mmm. Things haven't got that bad – yet!

Coach: So on a scale of zero to ten with ten representing you being completely confident that you can keep yourself safe and zero representing the opposite where would you place yourself at the moment?

Client: Six, six-to-seven?

Coach: And what is it that puts you at six, six-to-seven rather than lower?

Client: Well, I haven't given up completely! I still go in even though they'd probably wish I'd just go off sick.

Coach: What else?

The answer to each 'What else?' helps further establish the client's level of safety, the signs of safety, as well as informing both the client's and the coach's decision as to whether there is sufficient safety to permit no action being taken.

Coach: So on another scale of zero to ten with ten representing total confidence in keeping yourself safe and zero the opposite at least between now and when we next meet where would you rate yourself at present?

Client: Ten, definitely a ten! (*and laughs*)

The final decision is a difficult one and there are no absolute prescriptions. The coach's options will also vary from client to client. If a client has engaged the coach privately the coach may well have no access to the information needed to pass on concern about risk; then if the client does seem to be in danger of self-harm the coach can only do what he or she can do to persuade the client to allow access to their GP or a family member. In other situations the client might have been referred by an employer. This too is a difficult decision and may involve a breach of confidentiality in the face of a higher duty to protect life.

Summary

- The solution focused approach developed from the realisation that whatever the problem that clients bring there are always exceptions, exceptions that is to the rule of the domination of the problem in the client's life.
- Solution focus assumes that at these 'exception' times the client already has a small part of their preferred life and will therefore be interested to enquire how the client has been 'doing' these 'exception' times.
- Focusing on exceptions, however, involves the client thinking about and often describing the problem, in order to establish those times when it had not happened. This contradiction at the heart of the approach was resolved by solution focused coaches opening sessions by focusing on outcome, on the preferred future and then by inviting the client to identify those instances when elements of that preferred future are in place.
- Every client comes to coaching with both solution patterns as well as problem patterns in place. Every client has times when he has not 'done' his problem or indeed has 'done' a part of the preferred future.
- Whatever the question that the coach asks, the question always has to be fitting for the client, making sufficient sense to them in light of their current experiences. Thus although at times the client can manage to consider instances, at others, when the client is more problem dominated, the client is more likely to respond to exception questions, coping questions or even to thinking about how she is stopping things getting worse.

Activities: Histories of future success

Activity 1: Job skills (best done with a partner)

What are you good at in your job?
What else?
× 100 (advanced level)
× 50 (intermediate level)
× 35 (introductory level)

This exercise is a great confidence booster and the 'advanced' version, done before a job interview, will significantly enhance performance.

Activity 2: A sparkling moment (thanks to Michael White [2001], London)

- Think of a time when you shone, when you were proud to be you. It might have been a moment of kindness or generosity, courage or perseverance; it might have been a 'big' moment or a 'small' one. When you have remembered such a sparkling moment take a good look at yourself at that instant.
- What are you most pleased to recall about yourself in that moment? × 10
- What might others have noticed about you at that moment? × 6
- Which of the qualities you see in yourself at that moment are you most pleased to own?
- How has this quality shown itself in the past couple of weeks? × 5
- If you were to live life truer to that moment what difference would it make? × 5

6

Scales

The scale framework is the most flexible of the whole range of techniques that brief coaching makes available to the coaching process. It is able to encompass every aspect of the approach including the expectation of progress over time.

The simple zero to ten structure with ten representing the desired outcome and zero its opposite provides three conversational points of focus:

- a realistic description of a preferred future;
- an account of all that is currently contributing to that future, including past successes;
- an exploration of possible progress in the immediate future.

The solution focused scale

Although each and every question the solution focused coach will ask is hand-crafted to the specifics of the client's situation, tailored to fit the answers that the client has already given, the basic underlying structure of the scale question remains largely the same. Joelle comes to BRIEF feeling overwhelmed by the difficulties of finding her way forward in a highly competitive, externally glittering world, dominated by a small number of often charismatic male figures. In order to manage her situation she has found herself at times behaving, as she puts it, 'like a little girl', using a small voice, and concealing her real strengths and abilities. The session has already offered her space to describe, in detail, how she will know that she is managing her situation in a way that 'does her justice', in a way that fits with the person that she wants to be. Having constructed a detailed description based on this question the coach then asks 'On a scale of zero to ten, with ten representing you managing things at work in a way that does you full justice, in a way that you will be proud to look back on, and zero representing the opposite, where do you see things now?' This simple, yet flexible structure formed the basis for the rest of the work that was done with Joelle over four sessions.

Once the client has answered the opening 'best hopes' question the coach can therefore, if she chooses, set up a scale where ten represents the complete achievement of those hopes and zero the opposite (see Figure 6.1). A value for the current position and a 'good enough' outcome provide the rest of the 'scaffolding' for a conversation that could

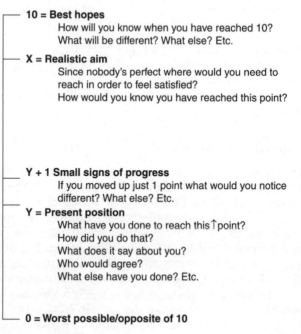

10 = Best hopes
How will you know when you have reached 10?
What will be different? What else? Etc.

X = Realistic aim
Since nobody's perfect where would you need to reach in order to feel satisfied?
How would you know you have reached this point?

Y + 1 Small signs of progress
If you moved up just 1 point what would you notice different? What else? Etc.

Y = Present position
What have you done to reach this ↑ point?
How did you do that?
What does it say about you?
Who would agree?
What else have you done? Etc.

0 = Worst possible/opposite of 10

Figure 6.1 The best hopes scale

include a description of 'ten', a description of all the evidence justifying the client's current self-rating, a description of everything the client has done to reach his current position and a description of what small signs will indicate a move of one point up the scale. The 'good enough' position then acts as a description of a way of knowing that enough work has been done and once it has been reached, the coaching, or that phase of the coaching is often complete.

One of the significant advantages of the scale framework is that it keeps the coach totally focused on the business in hand since every question is directly related to the purpose of the meeting. This might appear an unnecessary safeguard but it is surprising how tempted coaches can be to go 'sight-seeing' in their clients' lives. For a solution focused coach sight-seeing would include any curiosity about causation, any hypothesising about what might be 'at the bottom' of the problem, any interest in what might be blocking movement, any interest in an explanatory theory and any idea the coach might have about what the client should do. Steve de Shazer writes 'Too often people who want to learn solution focused brief therapy fall into the trap of not being able to see that the difficulty is to stay on the surface when the temptation to look behind and beneath is at its strongest' (Lee, Sebold and Uken, 2003: 18). Working in and with the client's account is indeed the greatest challenge for many who believe that their models give them privileged ways of making sense of people's behaviour, and an experience-based certainty about what people should do to resolve their difficulties. Once a scale has been set up it can remain the interviewing framework for the entire contract, returned to at each meeting until the contract is completed.

Constructing a scale

In the following example the coach has decided to start straight off with a scale. To some extent such decisions are arbitrary. On a busy day a coach might need to vary the structure of sessions simply in order to create variety and energy in his work. In this case, however, the client is very upbeat and confident and the coach is keen to capitalise on this. The scale offers the quickest route to identifying and making the most of this confidence: 'What puts you at two rather than lower?' At the same time the scale holds in mind the outcome focus of the work and later on can be used to help construct possible pathways towards this outcome.

Coach: What are your best hopes from our work together?

Client: I've just been promoted to sales manager and I want us to become the top sales team in the group – ambitious!

Coach: OK. So let's have a scale where ten equals you heading the top sales team in the group and zero means you wouldn't even have been shortlisted for the job. Where would you say you were at the moment?

Client: At the moment, not very high because a) it's not, to be frank, a team with a great performance and b) I've still got a lot to learn.

Coach: So where would you place yourself on the scale?

Client: About two!

Coach: And where would you need to reach to feel that even though it's not perfect you have done a job that you can be pleased with?

Client: Well, I'd like to get to ten but it's a big company so if we got into the top ten teams it would be a big achievement. So, let's say about eight.

Coach: So what is putting you at two rather than lower?

And so begins a detailed accounting of what is already a potential foundation for the client's future success. The skill of the coach will be in teasing out the fine detail of what has been achieved so far. This search could be divided into a number of areas:

- 'What have you done since you took up post that has contributed to you being at two rather than lower? What else?'
- 'What have you already learned about your team that tells you that your ambition is realistic? What else?'

This will focus the client on the team's skills and so encourage a solution focused approach to the client's leadership style.

Then there are the skills the client brought with him to the post.

- 'What do you think you brought to your interview that led the board to choose you for this post?'
- 'What else?' (× 20)

The possibilities for this historical exploration are virtually endless and might include descriptions of previously fulfilled ambitions, the personal and professional qualities that have proved useful in the past and past evidence of these qualities in action. By the end of this phase the client should be acutely aware of a very firm foundation for his ambition and have a strong sense of inevitability about further progress. When a coach decides to thoroughly investigate the foundations for future success already present he or she may take an entire session just for this phase and still expect the client to have made measurable progress by the next session. In most journeys knowing exactly how far you have come acts as an inspiration to take another step. Staying with the scale framework the coach might then choose to explore the client's hoped-for future.

- 'Let's say some months, or however long it takes, have gone by and you have just heard that your team has come through – you've just heard that they are the top team for that year! On that morning you take stock and think "What is it that makes this the best sales team in the organisation?" What would you be noticing about your team?'

When the qualities and achievements of the team have been detailed then time can be spent on the way the team was led.

- 'Looking at yourself as a leader what do you think you'll be seeing that fits with your current ambitions for yourself?'
- 'If your team was asked about your part in their success what do you hope they would be saying about you?'
- 'If the board were reviewing your progress what would they be seeing that justified their trust in you to do a good job?'

- 'And what would the board be remembering about you from the time of your appointment that led them to think this level of success was within your grasp?'

The client's 'good enough' position does not necessarily have to be detailed. To do so might have the effect of interfering with the client's ambition. Its purpose is to maintain a level of realism by acknowledging that success does not have to be absolute and 'perfection' is not the aim of coaching. The final phase, staying with the scale, is to chart out possible pathways towards the desired outcome. Here the brief approach offers its most serious challenge to many coaches.

Coach: If you moved up from two to three what might you notice different?

Client: There'd be fewer sales staff in the office.

Coach: What difference would that make?

Client: It would make a big difference – the office staff could get on with their work for one thing and for another sales aren't made from the office, not in our business anyway.

Coach: What would the office staff be noticing about you when this begins to happen?

Client: I'd probably be more relaxed! At the moment things are a bit tense. They've been stuck in their ways for years, some of them, and I know I can't just barge in but I think they know where I'm coming from and they are a bit on edge themselves so it's not easy.

Coach: How would the staff know that you are more relaxed?

Client: I'd probably be a bit more chatty – in fact I'd be more like what I'm trying to stop them doing!

Coach: And how will they know that you are more chatty and more relaxed because everyone is making progress rather than because you have given in?

Client: Because I'd be asking them how work things were going and it wouldn't sound like I was on their backs. Showing an interest in them. That sort of thing.

Coach: What difference do you think that might make?

Client: Quite a big one! In fact it will be a real sign of progress.

Coach: So what else will you be noticing that fits with such a big sign of progress?

Client: I'd start looking forward, or more looking forward to the day.

Coach: How will your partner know you are more looking forward to the day?

In this way the client builds up another layer of description that delineates what might be regarded as some of the probable signposts of progress. What the coach avoids doing is trying to turn any of these signs into targets or recommended steps. Whether or not any action is taken is entirely the client's business. Before examining this counter-intuitive decision a word about 'zero'.

A word about zero

An underlying assumption in solution focused thinking is that words create as well as describe the world. When we describe what we like (or dislike) about a person, group or situation we help to create and sustain that view. In a solution focused session a coach will avoid as much as possible using words that describe problems unless in doing so it would appear to the client that his difficulties were not being sufficiently acknowledged. In the following segment of a session, in which an extreme case of workplace conflict was resolved, the coach is very careful about which parts of the client's answers to include in the subsequent question.

Coach: What difference would that make?

Client: I wouldn't feel like punching him.

Coach: What would you feel like instead?

Client: I'd think that he's not a bad guy really and probably feel like talking to him.

Coach: And if you thought he's not a bad guy really and felt like talking to him what difference would that make to your journey into work?

Client: I wouldn't hate the idea of coming in.

Coach: Instead?
Client: I'd be more like I used to be, enthusiastic, wanting to get on.
Coach: And if you were more like you used to be, enthusiastic, wanting to get on, what might your colleague notice about you as you walked into the office?

With practice this selectivity about which parts of a client's answer to emphasise by repetition and which part to leave alone in order to avoid the risk of embedding them, becomes second nature to the brief coach.

It is for the same reason that a brief coach will rarely be specific about zero. The most common description is 'the opposite of ten' thus defining the problem in terms of the desired outcome. Another generic zero is 'the worst imaginable' although it is only likely to be used when there is some indication that things could actually be worse. Otherwise the client might answer 'zero'. Similarly, if there is evidence of progress the zero might be 'the worst things have ever been', which gives a good opening to asking the client how she has managed to improve her situation. However, if a client is feeling particularly hopeless the coach might have to acknowledge this more specifically. A client feeling so distressed he can barely get into work each morning might be invited to imagine zero as a 'never getting up for work again'.

One point up

Just as the brief coach will avoid inviting clients to describe the problem, or indeed zero directly, she will also take great care in how questions about moving up the scale are framed. She can either ask the client 'so given that you are already at a two on the scale what are you going to have to do to move one point up' (a 'steps' question) or alternatively she can ask 'so given that you are at a two, how will you know that you have moved just one point up the scale and reached three' (a 'signs' question). At first sight, avoiding even a hint of an action plan seems counter-intuitive; after all coaches are hired to make things happen and many coaches instinctively agree with Greene and Grant when they emphasise developing an action plan and concretising it by writing it down: 'Now we need to commit to action – thinking, wishing, wanting are not enough, we need to *do it!* and *start right now!* and *Put it in writing*' (Greene and Grant, 2003: 103). The difficulty with what might be regarded as 'steps to solution' questions (as opposed to 'signs of improvement happening' questions) is that the former imply that the client must *do* something, must take action. In some situations such a challenge will be counterproductive, serving merely to reconnect the client with a feeling of hopelessness 'that's the point I don't know what to do!' However, more generally the brief coach takes the view that inviting the client to specify and agree in advance specific actions that he will take is risky and often counterproductive.

The brief coach will trust that the client will be at least as informed by their answers as is the coach and therefore just as able to make action plans, or not. Moreover, if the coach is asking questions about how the client will know progress is being made without the added pressure on the client of having to follow through the words with actions then the client is likely to feel freer to answer. The more creative the client is in answering the more likely they are to generate useful (and for themselves) workable ideas.

Many clients initially express surprise when their descriptions of possible futures aren't immediately turned into targets, plans and tasks by the brief coach. Of these many are relieved and appreciative. In subsequent sessions the scale can be used to chart progress towards the desired outcome and serve as an indicator of when work can stop.

The possibilities for using scales are endless. A scale might be used as in the last example as a framework for the whole client–coach contract. Equally, one could be used for different aspects of the contract. In the course of a piece of work such as that above, separate scales could have been introduced to fine-tune the conversation. These might have related to different components of the task: getting the sales staff out of the office, being more relaxed with office staff, looking forward to coming to work, senior management's confidence in the client's ability, the level of sales and any other aspect of the contract that is viewed by the client as significant.

One very able client, Eva, was referred because of a serious shortfall in performance. For the first 26 minutes of the session the coach tried to establish a working contract but each time he asked 'What are your best hopes from this meeting?' Eva responded with: 'I don't know, and let me just tell you something else. . .' It was an understandable position: the client had had an unjustifiably difficult time in the organisation and a cynic's view would be that the referral had been made to avoid litigation. Promises of both support and training had apparently been made and broken, the management structure had been in disarray so very little guidance was available and such feedback that was given was always negative. This had gradually sapped the client's confidence, challenged her view of her self-efficacy, certainly undermined any possibility of job satisfaction and perhaps worst of all was having a deleterious effect on her family life. At the twenty-sixth minute the coach was given his first opening.

Client: . . . and the thing behind it all is that I'm not one of them and never will be and if they don't accept me ultimately I'm not going to get anywhere. So that's what needs to happen and how can it because I'll never be one of them!

Coach: So let me see if I've got this right – you think a starting point would be acceptance even though in one way you are not one of them . . .

Client: Yes, but I don't see that's going to happen!

Coach: OK. Yet if it did it would potentially be the start of something. It would potentially, at least, open things up?

Client: Yes, I think so anyway.

Coach: And if things began to open up, began to get resolved you might start seeing some changes for the better?

Client: Yes, but I suspect it's too late now.

Coach: And if there were some changes for the better you might reclaim some of your confidence?

Client: Yes because that has taken a big knock.

Coach: You might find yourself on some training courses?

Client: Yes.

Coach: You might be receiving more coherent support and guidance from your own managers?

Client: That would certainly be a change!

Coach: You might find yourself being more effective and enjoying your job more?

Client: Definitely!

Coach: And perhaps most important of all you would be able to get on with your family life more happily?

Client: Yes. Just a bit of balance really. At the moment I work all hours and when I'm not at work I'm worrying about work. It's no wonder they're all fed up of me!

Coach: OK, so balance – work–life balance?

Client: That's it exactly.

Coach: Let's see if we can get the measure of these factors. If we take the first, acceptance, and put it on a scale with ten being that you have all the acceptance you could want and zero being there is so little you would never have been appointed in the first place where would you say you are at the moment?

Client: That's a difficult one, you see, because it's not obvious and they'd never admit it but you just get the feel of it and I'll never have that education so I'm never going to be a member of their club!

Coach: So where would you say it was on the scale?

Client: Mmm. Two-to-three.

Coach: And where would you need to be to feel you had a good working level of acceptance as far as the job goes even though you can't join their 'club'.

Client: About seven.

Coach: OK. And if we scaled your self-confidence with ten being you couldn't wish for more and zero being you don't even have enough confidence to come into work where would you put yourself?

Client: Four.

The coach goes on to set up a scale for each part of the task: training, managerial support and guidance, effectiveness, job satisfaction and work–life balance. When each scale has been set up the coach returns to the first:

Coach: Coming back to the first scale, your degree of accept-
          ance, what tells you it's at two-to-three rather than
          lower?
Client: Well, they did employ me so that must say some-
          thing!
Coach: So what do you think they saw in you that led them
          to believe it was a good idea to get a 'non-club'
          member in to do the job?

The coach goes on to discover at least six or seven components of the existing level of acceptance before moving on to
the 'self-confidence' scale and doing the same there. This
will eventually lead to a list of forty to fifty 'items' already
working in the client's favour, probably far more than she
imagined at the start of the session. Each scale can then be
returned to briefly to find out two or three small signs of
progress with which to end the first session. If these signs of
progress are small enough it is likely that many are already
happening but have gone unnoticed. If this is the case then
immediate improvement is likely.

In the example above the entire session lasted 81 minutes
and proved to be the only one necessary. Although the client
continued to face difficulties at work she felt she could now
overcome them herself. Two years later Eva was reported to
be a well-respected member of the organisation.

Although scales can encompass the whole approach they
are more likely to be used alongside other 'techniques' most
typically after an exploration of the client's preferred future.
When the coach decides that a possible future has been
defined in sufficient detail he might go on to set up a scale.

- 'If we have a scale where ten stands for everything you
  have just described happening pretty much all of the time
  and zero is that none of it is happening where would you
  put things at the moment?'

Used in this way the main purpose of the scale will be to
discover as much as possible about aspects of the preferred
future that are already, even occasionally, in place. It might
also be used to trace out some of the more immediate possibilities that would indicate signs of progress.

Scale notes – making scales work for the client

It is important for the coach to bear in mind that scales are not mathematical realities, they simply provide a framework for solution focused questions and solution focused talking. They also belong to the client so should not be messed with or judged. If the client gives an unexpected number, too high or too low from the coach's point of view, the coach needs to see it as information to be accepted and accommodated rather than an interpretation that can be challenged. ('I would have put you higher than that' is a way for the coach to say he knows more about the client's life than the client does; in solution focused work this is not a good idea.) The solution focused coach will work hard to centralise the client's position and to 'marginalise' her own views and ideas, concentrating on the formulation of questions that fit with what the client wants from the coaching. If the client responds to a scale question in a first meeting with the answer 'well I'd say that I am at eight at the moment' it could well be relevant to ask 'so where would your line manager put things right now?' If the client responds with 'maybe two or three' the coach can enquire 'is this a problem to you?' and if the client says that it is indeed a problem a simple scale-based question opens up a future-oriented conversation 'so where would you need to be in her eyes for her to stop worrying about you?' Just sticking with the client and asking questions will be experienced by the client very differently from the coach centralising her own perspective, for example, 'Goodness I'd say things sound more like a two' and taking an expert defining position in the client's life.

A scale point is a great way for the client to tell the coach how bad things are without needing to go into the detail and sometimes it will have the opposite effect. Clients have at times described the most awful situations, enough to inspire despair in the most optimistic of coaches only to give a figure on the scale higher than they or the coach would have imagined. For a communication as simple as a single number it packs a lot of message.

Beware of trying to rush up the scale particularly when the client places themselves low. Remember that the scale is one of the best frameworks for finding out what the client is already doing that might contribute to the desired outcome and this information is like money in the bank (or treasure in the attic – there, potentially available but often forgotten). The coach is most in danger of trying to rush up the scale when he thinks that he is responsible for bringing about change, for sorting out problems, for getting things to happen rather than remembering that the coach's most powerful asset is merely his solution focused curiosity. Sitting back, helping the client gather her resources, knowing that there will always be some still to be discovered resource helps the coach stay in her own life rather than attempting to get inside the client's. Once this lesson has been learned the coach will begin to see that the more attention that is paid to what the client has already achieved the more likely the client is to take further steps: the more the history of the preferred future is created, for this is what the client and coach are doing, the more likely it is the preferred future will happen.

Despite this knowledge even an experienced coach will try to rush up the scale: the client says 'One' and instead of asking 'What is stopping it hitting zero?' the coach asks 'What will you need to do to get to two?' The coach will be informed (sometimes disdainfully) by the client of their mistake with a response like 'Well if I knew that don't you think I'd be doing it? Why do you think I'm here?' And it does us no harm to be reminded from time to time of our own stupidity.

Three useful scales

Confidence scaling

The creative coach will quickly learn to develop a range of scales, a repertoire that she will draw on repeatedly in her work. Beyond the simple 'best hopes' scale that forms the backbone of most solution focused interviewing the coach is likely to draw on confidence scaling, a formulation that invites the client into a listing of reasons to be confident. Towards the end of a session, very often after the client has already scaled where he sees himself in relation to his best hopes and therefore has articulated all the things that he is already doing that fit with the achievement of the best hopes for the work, the coach will ask:

- 'On a scale of zero to ten with ten standing for you having every confidence that you will indeed make progress towards your "best hopes" for our talking, and zero standing for the opposite, where would you put your confidence at this minute?'

Assuming that the client is not at zero on the scale, then answering the question will invite the client into formulating and then articulating everything that he knows about himself that is the basis for confidence. The more that the client develops a view of himself that fits with a confident expectation of achievement, the more likely it is that the client will make progress in the desired direction. Towards the end of a group session at BRIEF one of the members ends up by stating, just before they leave, 'we can do it, we can do it' and it is this response, not always of course said out loud, that the solution focused coach will be hoping for in the client.

Survival scaling

Every coach at some point will work with a client who is going through a very tough time. For people in such situations, whether they relate to external circumstances such as the responsibility for leading their organisation through recession, contraction and the need to make budget cuts or to more personal challenges, perhaps a disciplinary investigation or even facing the new responsibilities that come with a significant promotion, the most pressing necessity can sometimes be merely to survive, to keep going in the face of feeling overwhelmed. It is in these circumstances that the solution focused coach may choose to structure the focus for one meeting or more around the survival scale.

- 'On a scale of zero to ten with ten representing you getting through as well as anyone could given all the challenges and difficulties facing you at present, and zero representing the opposite, where would you put things at the moment?'

The scale invites the client to notice, most often, that he is not at zero, thereby allowing the client to challenge the frequent absoluteness of our condemnation of ourselves, 'I'm not coping *at all*', 'I'm not getting *anything* done', 'I feel like I've given up *totally*'. The bridge into possibility is offered by the coach's genuine and persistent curiosity about how come the client is wherever they are on the scale 'and not at zero'.

The scale of justice

Many of our clients may not feel overwhelmed but still may feel at times that they are not quite performing as they might hope, in a manner in other words that does them full justice. An awareness of potential that is not being fulfilled in their everyday performance leads to frustration and at times to self-criticism expressed at times in fairly vague language 'I just don't feel that I'm getting things together' or 'I always feel that I'm having to play catch-up, never quite getting it'. Using a scale in such circumstances will allow the client first to establish a platform, a solid base from which then to consider what signs of progress in relation to such a vague complaint might look like.

- 'On a scale of zero to ten with ten representing you performing at work in a way that does you full justice and zero representing the opposite of that, where do you see things at the moment?'

The coach can often usefully elaborate the structure of the scale by adding 'in a way that does you, your strengths, your skills and your capacities full justice', a more dramatic formulation that will invite the client to engage more fully with a sense of their potential. The more detailed the client's description of one point up the more likely it is that the conversation will be of use to the client and often it is useful to invite the client to imagine one point up in specific contexts to which they have alluded in outlining their complaint.

- 'So how will you know particularly in SMT [Senior Management team] meetings that you have moved just one point up?'

- 'What will your colleagues sitting with you at SMT meetings be noticing about the way that you are participating that will fit with you being just one point up?'
- 'As you present the working of the development subgroup to the board what will be all the signs, to you and to others, that will tell you that you have moved another point towards ten?'

An easy way for the coach to establish peak performance moments is simply to ask the client

- 'And where is the highest that you have been on that (doing yourself justice) scale over the past month?'

Exploring with the client that peak moment, the external manifestations, the internal experience, the thoughts and actions that accompanied it, will often serve to increase the potential repeatability for the client.

Multi-scales

Sometimes our clients seem totally overwhelmed and if we are not careful it is a feeling any coach can catch. One middle-aged man referred by his employer responded to the 'best hopes' question with: 'To be honest I can't see what you can do. I don't like my job, I don't like my boss, I don't like my colleagues, I've had all my confidence sapped, I have no prospects and my marriage is just about on the rocks. Can you sort that out?'

The temptation is either to lose hope immediately or ask the client to 'prioritise'. The second option is logical but not often useful. Here is a client weighed down by a sack of problems he barely has the strength to carry into the room. He will already have tried to sift through them, organise and prioritise them all to no avail as they are so interlocked they seem impossible to deal with individually. In response the coach says, in effect, you might be carrying that load but don't expect me to, I'm just a one-problem-at-a-time coach. Fortunately, a solution focused coach can handle as many problems as the client can bring. In response to the client's rhetorical question 'Can you sort that out?' the coach answered: 'Well, I'm sure that between us we could have a pretty good try! Do you want to get going?'

Rather taken aback the client said 'Sure!' and waited.

The coach replied: 'So let's see if we can get the measure of all this: if I've heard right you would like to enjoy your job, have a better relationship with your boss, your colleagues and your wife, you'd like to get your confidence back and see the possibility of better prospects ahead?'

'In a nutshell, yes' the client responded, now intrigued.

The rest of the session followed a well-worn solution focused trail: each issue had its own scale and although the client was low on most of them it was only a matter of persistence to find ten or so ways the client was preventing himself being even lower on the scale. This produced a list of between sixty and seventy positive elements in the client's situation. Two or three very small signs of progress added a list of almost twenty realistic possibilities for the future. A little time was then taken to interweave the scales 'If you moved up one point on the "regaining confidence" scale what difference might that make to the "getting on better with your boss" scale?' A few such questions created the possibility of the vicious cycle he came with turning into the sort of virtuous cycle where an improvement in any circumstance will have a positive impact on every other circumstance. The client's parting comment was 'On the way here I felt totally weighed down, I couldn't see anything positive! But it's not that bad really, is it?' He thought he could manage without further sessions and did. His organisation continued to refer.

Summary

- Scales questions are flexible and can be used as a way of facilitating all of the core conversations that the solution focused coach wants to invite the client to explore.
- Solution focused scales make it easy for the coach to elicit everything that the client is already doing that fits with the preferred future.
- Solution focused scales represent a simple way of highlighting the progress that the client has already made.

- It is important to remember that the particular answer that the client gives is less important than the possibilities for conversation that the scale questions permit.
- Scales are best informed by the coach's solution focused curiosity about the potential and actual evidence relating to the client's particular responses happening, rather than as a basis for 'action planning'.

Activities

Activity 1: The coach that you aspire to be

- On a scale of zero to ten, with ten standing for the coach that you aspire to be and zero representing the furthest from ten that you can imagine, where do you see yourself now on that scale?
- What is it that tells you that you are at that point on the scale and not at zero? (Make a list of at least twenty pieces of 'evidence'.)
- What do others see you doing that contributes to you being at that point on the scale? (Remember that 'others' might be the clients with whom you work, colleagues, your supervisor, anyone in fact with whom you come in touch during the course of your work. List at least five pieces of evidence for each of these 'stakeholders'.)
- How will you know that you have moved just one point up on your scale?
- What will you notice yourself doing differently when you have moved one point up? (Make a list of eight signs.)
- What will others notice you doing that is different when you have moved one point up? (Make a list of at least four signs for each of these 'stakeholders'.)

Activity 2: Project yourself

- Bring to mind a project or an intention that is current in your life.
- On a scale of zero to ten, with ten representing your project confidently achieved and zero standing for the moment

when you first took on the project or formulated the intention, where do you see yourself at present?
- What is it that tells you that you are at that point on the scale
  and not at zero? (Make a list of twenty pieces of evidence.)
- What have you done and what have you drawn on to get to
  where you are?
- How will you know that you have moved just one point up
  on your scale? (List at least ten signs of possible progress.)
- On a scale of zero to ten, with ten standing for complete
  confidence and zero standing for the opposite, how confident are you of making progress with your project (of
  moving forward with your intention)?
- What is it that you know about yourself that gives you that
  much confidence?

7

Closing a session

A solution focused summary

Traditionally, solution focused sessions have ended with the coach delivering compliments based on the information provided by the client. The coach will pick out aspects of the client's account to be 'impressed' by or 'admiring' of and if possible attribute positive qualities to the client such as courage, perseverance, loyalty and concern. In effect the coach gives an opinion, albeit the best opinion possible in the circumstances. As will be seen below, in giving compliments it is important that they conform to certain criteria: they need to be genuine, based on evidence provided in the session, they should be specific, pertinent to the matter in hand and they must be something with which the client can agree. Sweeping generalisations, unfounded flattery and contradictions to the client's own view will cast serious doubt about the coach's genuineness and skill. However, the original purpose of these compliments makes them less benign than they look. It was to produce a 'yes-set', a semi-trance in which the client, having agreed with all that had been said then went on to agree to whatever task the coach might set. Compliments are, therefore a hangover from the early influences of Ericksonian hypnotic techniques.

BRIEF has long had mixed feelings about compliments. When asked their view, clients almost invariably appreciate them yet they do not sit well with the underlying principles of the approach. If everything the coach does and conveys through the entire session is related to the client's own knowledge and expertise what sense does it make for the coach to then express not just his own opinion but to express it as the closing words thus giving it maximum importance? Since we believe that the difference coaching makes is made through the conversation it is hard to believe that a closing declaration counts for anything except perhaps for a very temporary feel-good sensation in the client and an experience of benevolence in the coach.

With these thoughts in mind brief coaches will normally give a summary of the conversation rather than obvious compliments. This summary will pay particular attention to the desired future and anything already contributing to it. The coach will also acknowledge whatever difficulties the client is facing but in a way that affirms the client's accept-ance of the challenge. For example, summarising the first session with Eva (described in Chapter 6):

Coach: No one could deny you have a challenge on your hands, in fact, more than one challenge – a whole basket of them! Yet not only have you not given up, you have maintained a tenable position on each one: you have held your head up even though not sure of your acceptance and even though your confidence and sense of effectiveness has been knocked you have been able to take stock and tell yourself you're OK. You haven't given up on your ambitions for yourself and you've taken a pretty crucial step to sort things out at home. You've also got some clear ideas about what you are looking for in future: a bit more 'corridor chat' with your colleagues, a response from your training director even if it is just to say 'no', finding a way, possibly with a joke, to take issue with the colleague who's been undermining and, maybe most important of all, having some ideas about moving things forward with your partner.

In formulating the summary the solution focused coach will be paying careful attention to a number of key guidelines which are associated with the summary being useful.

1 Be careful not to add new material at this stage, simply emphasise material that has already been agreed and

accepted during the course of the session. The last thing that the coach wants at the end of a session is for the client to take exception to something that has been included and to begin to differ either by openly arguing or challenging, or by becoming privately critical of the coach's understanding of the situation. Similarly, stay as close as is possible to the language and the expressions that the client has already used. Implanting our own words, at any point in the session and certainly in the summary, risks rejection. Far better and less risky to echo back to the client the words that he or she has provided us with as these are most likely to be acceptable.

2   Ensure that the client's predicament has been sufficiently acknowledged for her to feel open to constructive feedback. If the client feels underacknowledged then when the coach highlights achievement she will often be tempted to remind the coach of just how tough things are, possibly thinking that the coach is not fully appreciating the difficulties. This is the last thing that the solution focused coach would want at this stage of the session, a reversion on the part of the client into problem-talk, and a reversion that could easily have been avoided if the coach had found the right balance.

3   The solution focused coach will always work from what can be termed a 'yes and . . .' position rather than a 'yes but . . .' position. The difference is crucial. When the client criticises his own performance and appears to be mired in hopelessness the temptation for the coach is to attempt to rescue the client by arguing with him, adducing evidence that what he is saying is not the whole truth. If the coach prefaces his rescue attempt with the word 'but' then the client is challenged either to give up his own perception and accept that the coach is right, or to hold on to his own perception in the face of the challenge, often feeling obliged to bring forth new evidence to support his case. The word 'but' is an exclusive word, since either one thing is right *or* the other, not both. However, when the coach begins her responses to the client from the 'yes and . . .' position the coach is accepting the client's statement and in the context of that acceptance inviting the client to

become curious about another, often previously unnoticed, feature of his situation. It is the acceptance, the working *with* rather than the challenging and confronting that makes it easier for the client to put his curiosity to work in a way that will be potentially productive for him. Thus if the client states that he has had a terrible fortnight the solution focused coach will move first to acceptance:

- 'Sounds like things have been really tough over the past few weeks and given that – given just how tough things have been – I can't help noticing that somehow you have still managed to complete the half-yearly review, present it to SMT not just coherently but persuasively in a way that won you plaudits, and in addition you have managed to support Dave in his struggles with legal?'

So it is important to remember in the summary that the coach is not attempting to convince the client or to argue with him, merely to summarise the things that the client has said that seem associated with the possibility of progress in the context of an acceptance of the client's position. A short-hand way of reminding ourselves of this is: 'yes and . . .' not 'yes but . . .'

4   Take care not to overwhelm your client with too much material. Prioritise and select the material that relates most closely and directly to the issue that the client has brought to the table. A useful idea to remember when formulating a summary is that less is often better than more, a smaller number of relevant and well-chosen comments being more effective than an unfocused outpouring of enthusiasm for the client and his capacities.

5   Check throughout the feedback that the client is in agreement with the summary being offered. The client may be nodding in agreement or may be verbally indicating agreement. If this is not happening ask the client 'Does this make sense to you?', 'Does this do you justice?', 'Am I missing something here?' A negative answer gives the coach a short amount of time to adjust her position or tone or maybe merely to apologise and undertake to do a better job next time.

Although BRIEF is moving away from compliments as an end of session ritual they still have a place in the overall work. Part of the coach's task in managing the conversation is to invite the client into new perspectives that at times will throw a more positive light on experience. A client may describe facing down a hostile colleague. A crudely solution focused coach might give a straight compliment such as 'that shows you have courage' but a more sophisticated coach will frame the idea as a question either tentatively: 'Did that take courage?' or more forcefully if there is enough background information to support the assumption, 'how did you find the courage to take such a difficult step?' By placing the compliment in a question it can be accepted or rejected by the client without undermining the coach's credibility.

Suggestions

In the early days of the solution focused approach tasks took a central place (de Shazer, 1985). Sessions were designed to elicit information pertinent to task construction and the model's assumption was that change came about as a result of the client carrying out the task that had been prescribed. The task was the behavioural equivalent of the medicine and needed to be swallowed, hopefully with good grace. The early literature (Dolan, 1991; Berg and Miller, 1992) is full of task descriptions that owe much to the influence of Milton Erickson from whose work neurolinguistic programming (NLP) was developed. The tasks that Erickson designed, and the ones developed by de Shazer, are almost always indirect in that they never ask the client to do the obvious. Their purpose is to activate the client's own solution-finding processes rather than to generate a specific solution. They will involve pretending, coin tossing, predicting and behaving differently on different days. Fun as they are to devise they belong to a time when the coach trusted the client less and made himself more central than we would now regard as necessary.

Even less direct and less intrusive were the noticing or observation tasks in which the client would be asked to notice anything that happens that the client would like to continue to have happen. This was meant to divert the client's attention from what is wrong to what is right since the latter provides a more creative platform for positive action.

As BRIEF began to attach more significance to the conversation between coach and client, and in line with giving precedence to the client's rather than the coach's expertise, task giving was largely abandoned. Subsequent research showed no difference in outcome in cases where no task had been given. This in itself is justification for abandoning tasks altogether. However, there are times when the client has declared a definite wish for something to do (and times when the coach cannot restrain herself!) when at least a suggestion is appropriate. Making a suggestion, rather than giving a task, requires special attention to language. The words we use to describe what we are doing always have the potential to trap us, to lead us in directions that we had not expected. If the coach, at the end of a session were to 'give the client homework' or if she were to 'prescribe a task', the hidden logic of these ways of describing what we are doing can get us into difficulties. Both concepts, 'giving homework' or 'prescribing tasks' come with built-in relational implications, and the implied relationships are markedly hierarchical. Only someone in a more powerful relational position can 'give homework' to someone who is relationally less powerful, for example the teacher to the pupil, the guru to the neophyte. And what happens when people fail to do their homework? Historically and traditionally they get into trouble. Now clearly the coach is never in a position to dole out punishments, but nonetheless the repercussions of failing to carry out homework can be risky to the client. The coach can begin to think differently about the client; the coach can begin to develop certain ideas about the client that are unlikely to be helpful to the solution focused process, namely that the client might be 'unmotivated' or even 'resistant'. Ideas such as these interfere with the basis for cooperation that is fundamental to the solution focused approach, trapping the coach, leading her into the danger of instrumental, even confrontational, thinking. The coach can begin to reflect on the need to 'get the client motivated', or to 'deal with the client's resistance'. The stepping away from the client's position and seeing the client as someone who needs the coach to 'act on them' rather than 'work with them', fundamentally undermines the solution focused modus operandi.

So if the coach does form the view that some sort of formal intervention is required, how this is formulated is important. The framing that fits the solution focused approach best is to think of these interventions as suggestions. The coach can *offer* a *suggestion*. And naturally if the client chooses not to make use of the suggestion then the coach will be lead to turn the spotlight on herself and her work rather than on to the client. What was wrong with the way that I framed that suggestion? In what way did it not fit the client's situation? What have I learnt from this that would inform me if I were to offer this client another suggestion in future? The voluntary element of the transaction can be highlighted by the way that the suggestion is framed. For example the coach can frame the suggestion in such a way that the danger of a critical impact on the relationship if the client chooses not to use the coach's idea is minimised:

- 'Here's an idea that you might find useful. Don't worry if you have too much on your plate. Don't worry if you forget and just ignore it if it does not make sense to you. However, if you do have the time and the energy and if this makes sense to you, what I suggest is that you might like, over the course of the next 2 weeks, just to watch out for the times that you notice yourself being confident in a way that is right for you and good for the team. From what you have been saying during the course of our meeting today it just seems that you might discover something useful from this.'

However the client responds to this can now more easily be framed by the coach as cooperation, an outcome whose likelihood is further increased if the coach remembers to abstain from following-up the task at the beginning of the next session with a question that will often feel to the client a little like 'so have you done your homework?' An idea in solution focused coaching is that each session, as we shall see, is treated as an independent entity. Although Steve de Shazer, to the end of his therapeutic life, loved the cleverness of tasks and regularly, indeed probably routinely, used them he did almost invariably describe them as experiments, saying to the client 'I think that you may learn something interesting from this'. This avoided any sense or implication that the tasks were intended to be curative of the client and maintained the idea that in solution focus people find their own solutions rather than somehow being sorted out by the clever coach. In solution focused coaching all the credit needs to be with the client and genuinely so.

The most typical suggestion that a solution focused coach might offer to a client is a minimally intrusive 'noticing' suggestion based on some of de Shazer's early work. These are those suggestions aimed at directing the client's attention towards what is working. These might include more *general* forms of noticing:

• notice whatever you do that works;
• notice any sign of your hoped-for future beginning to happen;
• notice what you are doing when you begin to see yourself moving up the scale.

Or more *specific* to the client's situation and hopes:

• watch out for those times that you feel irritated with him and you deal with the irritation in a way that seems right for you and OK for him;
• notice the times when you feel a little more energised by life and figure out what's different at those times;
• notice the times when you feel that you are getting the balance right between life and work and how you are doing that.

Offering clients suggestions such as these, which refocus the client's patterns of noticing, fit with the shift that is discernible more generally within the solution focused process. It can be argued that what we notice as we go around our worlds is the inevitable basis for us to reach certain identity conclusions (White, 2001), and if what we pay attention to and thereby selectively notice is everything that goes wrong for us this will lead to identity conclusions that might serve to make positive changes in our lives more difficult. However, there is little research-based evidence that would prove that these suggestions in themselves make a difference and thus they remain an option to solution focused coaches, some of whom will feel drawn towards them and some of whom, acting on a principle of minimalism, doing the least that is nonetheless consistent with a good outcome, will not.

More about compliments

Solution focused coaching is as multi-layered as it is simple. As the coach searches for the client's strengths, resources, competencies, capabilities and successes he will be storing what he finds not just for the closing summary but also as material for further questioning:

- 'Could I just go back to something you said earlier about not being the sort of person to give up easily? Tell me a bit more about how that has stood you in good stead.'

But there is another reason for looking for what's working and looking for value in the client. Occasionally, the coach will be faced with a reluctant client, most likely someone who has been 'told' to attend and who sees the coach as part of a hostile management. In these circumstances the client has little reason to cooperate more than minimally with the process: if he thinks the coach is 'out to get him' then he would be unwise to give anything away! A solution focused coach will respect this position and from the outset be looking for ways to convey his good intentions to the client. The simplest way to do this is with a compliment.

- To an 'outspoken' client: 'You're certainly an outspoken person – a great quality to have though I bet you're not always thanked for it!'
- To a client with a negative account of his treatment: 'I have to say that a lot of people would have given up in the face of that! How have you managed to hang in there despite the pressure?'
- To a client who feels he has no choice: 'So it's your commit-ment to your family, your children and their education that keeps you putting one foot in front of the other?'

The effect of compliments like these can be dramatic often leading the client to put his or her whole weight behind the coaching process. If an explanation for this phenomenon was to be found it is likely not to be in the compliment itself but in the evidence to the client, expressed through the compliment, that the coach is listening in a very different way to that which was expected. And this is where the solution focused discipline and the giving of compliments come together.

Elements of a good compliment

If we think of compliments we have received and those in particular that have made a difference, we quickly realise there is more to a good compliment than meets the eye. A good compliment must fulfil a number of important criteria including the following.

1 It must be meant, the giver must be honest.
2 It must be evidence based. If the receiver was to ask, the giver must be able to give 'chapter and verse' for its justification.
3 It must be pertinent to the relationship between receiver and giver and appropriate to the purpose of that relationship: remarking on a client's hairstyle is unlikely to be an appropriate compliment from a coach but perhaps essential from a good friend.
4 It must be unconditional – without strings. The compliment isn't a backdoor attempt at getting the client to do something. It should stand freely whatever the client's future behaviour with no price tag attached.
5 It must be in some way significant to the client and the business they have with the coach. A compliment to a creative director about their artistic flare will not necessarily be significant in a conversation about how they might better deal with a 'difficult' member of staff.
6 It must be something the client can agree with and most certainly not a way for the coach to claim greater knowledge of the client than the client him or herself might have.

7 And it must be delivered in a way that the client can hear:
   a 'tough' client might only hear a 'toughly' worded compliment whereas a thoughtful client might need to be
   matched with thoughtfulness.

To match these exacting requirements the coach must both
listen carefully and, more specifically, listen for whatever the
client says that might in some way help define the purpose,
describe the desired outcome or be evidence of that outcome
being possible. It is the evidence of this listening rather than
the compliment itself that is likely to convince the client
that the coach is genuinely interested in a real contract –
one that is led by the client rather than by the agenda of the
coach or employer.

During any session a coach is likely to go off track or be
misunderstood in a way that leads the client to think about
withdrawing cooperation. It is these times that a brief but
genuine compliment fulfilling all the above criteria is likely
to bring the client back on board.

A client had been describing the difference that feeling
more confident would make to his performance at a management meeting. He suspected, possibly wrongly, that there
were concerns about how he was managing his own group
and was unsure if the offer of coaching was less than benign.

Coach: And if you'd had a meeting like that what would you
          notice about yourself as you left?
Client: I'd feel great!
Coach: How would you know?
Client: A spring in my step – whistling a happy tune!!
Coach: And when you got back to your section how would
          they know you had got your confidence back?
Client: They wouldn't.
Coach: If they did?
Client: They wouldn't. I don't let any of this affect how I am
          with them. I'm always upbeat; I don't let them see
          what's going on inside. No they're not affected.

The client has turned from a humorous enjoyment of his self-
description to a less than humorous 'defence' of his leadership.
The coach wonders if the client has misunderstood the purpose

of the question and read it as a ploy to get him to admit that his behaviour is in some way problematic to the team. On the other hand the client might just be being straightforward. Faced with a choice like this the solution focused coach will stay with the 'surface'. Trying to second-guess what a client might 'really' mean is a sure way to derail the session. On the other hand the coach cannot fail to recognise a change in tone from collaborativeness to carefulness. To accommodate this and attempt to build a bridge back to collaboration the coach will try to give a compliment as well as taking the client at face value. In this way he hopes the client will accept his genuine wish to work towards the client's best outcome.

Coach: OK, so as far as your group goes you have remained on the ball and not let these difficulties you are having elsewhere detract from that?

Client: That's right.

Coach: How have you managed to do that? I know it's what a good manager should do but the gap between what we should do and what is possible can sometimes be too wide – how have you still managed to bridge it?

Client: With difficulty, because to be honest I have sometimes come down from the top floor and just wanted to put my head in my hands!

Coach: So how have you kept your end up with your own group at those times?

Client: I just do and then when I get the chance I lock myself away so they can't see me.

Coach: That takes some doing! So what would you notice about yourself when you rejoined your group after such a successful meeting?

Client: I wouldn't want to shut myself away!

Coach: Instead?

Client: Instead? I'd probably hang around a bit more, maybe talk about the meeting if it wasn't confidential; just be a bit more relaxed.

Coach: Would they like that – you hanging around a bit more, letting them in on the meeting and so on?

Client: Yes, I think so – if I was relaxed, that is.

Coach: How would you know that they liked it?

Client: Oh, someone would say something – make a joke, something like that!
Coach: Would you be pleased they'd noticed and responded?
Client: Absolutely, because however hard you try to hide it they're not fools, they know something is going on.

The client has been taken seriously and the questions have also contained affirmative statements or compliments. His response has been to resume collaboration. Instead of seeing the relationship between himself and his group as an arena for criticism and therefore a dangerous place to go he has, within a few answers, seen it as an area of potential resource and future development.

One of BRIEF's answers to the dilemma of compliment giving is to embed them in questions. In the example above the 'How did you manage to do that?' questions contain a compliment about the client's achievement and when the client says 'With difficulty' there is a sense that he has heard and valued the appreciation. On the other hand it also gives the client a chance to question the coach. One client referred because a domestic crisis was having a serious impact on his work was asked the following question.

Coach: How on earth do you still manage to get up and go to work in the mornings?
Client: Of course I'm going to do that! It's going home that's the difficulty!

In this case the coach had got the embedded compliment in the wrong place and the client both challenged this and was kind enough to give the coach guidance as to where to place his appreciation!

Summary

- At the end of a solution focused conversation the coach will offer the client a summary, including in the summary what she has heard the client say that fits with the likelihood of the client achieving his best hopes for the work.
- Summaries tend to be founded on acknowledgement of the client's situation, genuine acknowledgement allowing the

client to relax and be more open to the essentially optimistic material included.

- In framing her summary the coach will stay as close as
possible to what the client has actually said, using as far
as possible the client's own words.

- The solution focused coach is less likely now than in the
early days of the approach to offer compliments, that is,
strengths-related feedback not contained within the
client's responses to questions asked. These can at times
be embedded in the questions that the coach will ask.

- While there has been a long history of prescribing tasks
at the end of sessions, the BRIEF approach has minimised
this and is most likely, if at all, to offer a minimally impo-
sitional noticing suggestion.

Activities: Appreciative feedback

Activity 1: Characteristics of a good compliment

Think of a compliment you have received at some point in your
life that you think might have made a positive difference to how
you thought about yourself. What made this such an influential
compliment? If this is done as a group everyone can share their
compliments and then draw up a list of the characteristics of a
good compliment. The list can then be compared with the list
in this chapter.

Activity 2: Constructing a good compliment

Think of three colleagues, one to whom you are close to and
whom you value, a more distant colleague you admire and a
colleague with whom you experience difficulty.

Write down, in a form of words that could actually be
spoken to the person (although they don't have to be spoken)
a compliment that fits the criteria of a good compliment for
each of the three. Obviously the last will be the most difficult
and also the most enlightening.

8

Second and subsequent sessions

Following up improvements

Subsequent sessions are often like first sessions in reverse. Unless one contracted piece of work is over and another begun, or unless each session is seen as a stand-alone event (in which case the session will resemble a first session with best hopes, preferred future and instances of the preferred future already in place), then the opening question will be 'What's better?', 'What's progressed?' or any other question related to the purpose and that carries an assumption of progress. This is not an overly optimistic question but one that reflects the most likely outcome of the previous session: things are likely to have improved and if they haven't it reflects as much on the efficacy of the coach as it does the actions of the client.

The purpose of the question is to begin a new search for everything the client has done that might contribute to their preferred future. This will mainly relate to what they have done since the last session but it is also likely to extend back from that as new information about long-standing resources, capabilities and achievements come to light. The more detailed the descriptions of what the client has done successfully the more these actions will become part of his or her everyday repertoire.

Even the smallest and most temporary improvements deserve exploration because it is these that will give the best clues to behaviours that are worth expanding. A client will often refer to a change and then minimise its significance.

Client: Yes, things did improve for a couple of days but on Monday they were right back to normal.

Coach: So what was different in those couple of days?

Client: I don't know; she was just more polite. But she's back where she was with a vengeance this week!

Coach: How was she more polite?

Client: She actually asked me how I was which took me right by surprise!

Coach: Were you pleased?

Client: When I got over the shock I was, yes.

Coach: How do you think she could tell you were pleased?

Client: Easily – I offered to make her a cup of tea!

The coach will be careful to avoid minimising the client's disappointment and even more careful not to miss the potential goldmine of information to be found in this 2-day period of improvement. At the same time the coach must be careful not to become overenthusiastic about the improvement. As the description of the two days unfolds and the parts played by the client and her colleagues become more explicit it is apparent that much of the client's preferred future is a concrete possibility. In the first session the client had jokingly said that making her colleague a cup of tea would be a sign of progress almost unimaginable. By the second session the cup of tea was already a real part of her history. Many other features of the client's imagined description had become a reality while others had been adjusted in the light of experience:

- 'I suppose she's never going to be a diplomat; she just doesn't see it. But at least you know where you are with her and that's more than can be said of some people!'

If a change can last for a day it can last for two or ten. The more clearly it is described the more likely it is to be repeated. And once progress has been described the coach and client can begin to describe what signs of further progress might look like. In this way the second and subsequent sessions will begin with immediate history, progress since the last session, and close with next small signs of the preferred future happening.

Ideally then, all the sessions after the first are *follow-up*. There is rarely a need to explore a second time a client's preferred future in the sort of detail that was paid to it in the first session, but this may be done if the client's first description was not specific enough or if the client appears to have changed his view of what he is seeking. A typical questioning sequence would be as follows.

Follow-up to improvements

What's been better since we last met?

This question reasonably presupposes change. Although we avoid presuppositional questions that are designed simply to create a positive mindset we do use them if the embedded assumption is well founded. 'What's better?' reflects a strong likelihood or, as nothing remains constant, the inevitability of change. The coach's task is to tease out these changes and explore their impact on the client's life. Occasionally the client will not be able to think of any change for the better and might even report a worsening of their circumstances. Later we will examine a number of ways to respond many of which lead eventually to evidence of improvement. Once each improvement is identified its significance can be amplified by further rigorous questioning.

What did you do?

This begins an enquiry that seeks to enable the client to define the *detail* of progress in such a way that she can understand her part in it and therefore take more control over her life. Sometimes it is not easy for the client to remember anything, especially if the intervening period has been a difficult one. The coach needs to remain confident that every client will have done *something*.

How did you do it?

Once again it might require gentle perseverance on the part of the coach to help the client identify her own part in any changes that have taken place. This is a question that invites the client to identify positive qualities as well as constructive actions. The identification of constructive actions increases the client's sense of ownership in relation to the changes, supporting the client's idea that she did something that was associated with the change happening, while at the same time increasing the potential 'repeatability' by the client of the action. Eliciting the positive qualities underlying the actions invites the client to redescribe herself in possibility terms, thus gently challenging the tendency of clients very often to describe themselves in relation to their limitations, stories of self that inhibit the client's sense that he is able to take control of his life in a positive way. These qualities can then be used to generate further ideas about action; for example 'if this quality were to be brought to bear on your relationship with your manager what do you think you'd notice?'

What did others see you doing?

The client, by seeing herself through the eyes of others, develops a still richer description. Clients often remark how useful it is to see themselves at their best through the eyes of others. Being specific about particular 'others', for instance 'which of your colleagues do you think was the first to notice?' brings the client's strengths and possibilities much more into focus.

What have you learned about yourself?

Once again the client is asked to consider how each success reflects on their sense of identity and the consequent expectations they have of themselves. A socially isolated person might discover social skills of which they were hitherto unaware: 'I hadn't realised that people were interested in me – I like it so much I sometimes worry I've gone too far the other way!' It may also be useful to ask what difference particular changes have made to other areas of the client's life: 'So what difference has getting on better with your boss made to how things have been going at home?' Inviting the client to comment on themselves as if they were talking about another person can be a very useful means to bring this new self-knowledge to light. One client described in a very off-hand minimising way a week of extraordinary achievements. When asked: 'If you were listening to the radio and heard someone describing what you have just described what do you imagine you would think of her achievement?' she was able to reply: 'Well, actually, put like that, I'd think she was extraordinary!'

Exploring success is not as easy as it seems. Coaches tend to prefer fixing problems and planning out futures rather than excavating success, and much value can be lost by moving on too quickly. Every success is a potential foundation for future progress: the stronger the foundation the greater the load it will bear. But when each seam of progress has been finally exhausted the coach can then turn her attention to the future.

What would be the next small signs of progress?

The process is almost complete: a thorough investigation of what the client has done leads to a consideration of what they *might* notice in the near future. Just as in the first session the more mundane and detailed the description the more impact the conversation is likely to have.

The most obvious framework for this exploration of past success and future possibilities is the scale. Not only does it help keep the focus pertinent to the original contract but it provides a client-centred tool of measurement that shows not only progress but also when to stop.

When things are the same or worse

A coach's heart might sink even at the thought of a client saying things are the same or even worse but it happens so best to be prepared. First of all the coach must take heed of the client's mood and avoid any possibility of minimising their disappointment or even hopelessness. A too vigorous launch into standard solution focused questions is likely to leave the client behind and when the questions are asked the tone needs to be right. This comes with experience. What every coach will also learn with experience is the number of times a client says nothing has changed but by the end of the session has discovered more changes than they could have hoped for. The message from this is that to see things we sometimes have to look for them and when a client has been through troubled times and has had to 'watch their back' they don't always notice the change of scenery in front.

Twenty minutes into a second session where no change has been reported the coach has been asking the client how she has at least kept things on an even keel. This is hard work.

Coach: And what did you notice about this morning that gave you confidence that at least things weren't going to get worse?

Client: This morning wasn't so bad really.

Coach: How come?

Client: I had a good night's sleep – that always helps!

Coach: What do you think led to having a good night's sleep?

Client: I don't know. Actually, I have been sleeping better.

Coach: Since?

Client: For about the past week, I think. Not every night, but most nights. Yes, I suppose that's an improvement!

Coach: So how did you get it to happen?

Client: I don't know – I don't think I did anything special.

Coach: What do you think it might have been?

Client: We had a weekend away. Maybe that had something to do with it.

Coach: If it was the weekend away what was it about the weekend that might have led to you sleeping better?

Client: It was actually a lovely weekend and for the first time I managed to put work out of my mind and just get on with it – and on the way back I thought work isn't everything! Maybe that was it.

Coach: In most people's books sleeping well is a big thing –

Client: Absolutely!

Coach: – and it looks like you brought that about in a pretty creative way! So what difference is it making?

Client: Actually, now I think of it, a big difference.

The client goes on to describe numerous small changes in her life at work and at home, differences which individually were not hugely significant but cumulatively showed real change over a broad front. On the lookout to stop a difficult situation worsening she had not noticed, or not noticed the significance, of the many small signs of progress.

When the client reports no change the first line of enquiry is usually to become interested in what they have done to maintain stability or to stop things getting worse. This demands great discipline on the part of the coach who might be prone to feeling disappointed both with himself and with the client and who might also feel pressurised to be more interventive and to try harder to push things forward thereby abandoning the meticulous sifting that is the basis for every solution focused conversation. The process could be compared with an archaeological dig where a piece of ground is being carefully sifted but with little to show. Occasionally a fragment of pottery is unearthed but closer inspection shows it to be a part of a Woolworth's cup rather than a Roman vase. If the team abandon their search at this point they risk never finding a series of more promising fragments or even a complete vase. A client on summing up her experience of work at BRIEF described the process 'as like a long treasure hunt' and then she added a piece of advice that most coaches need to hold onto when things are difficult: 'you have to dig deep'. What is certain is that without the careful digging nothing will be found.

When things are worse

It is not often that a client will report a worsening situation but when they do it can be one of the few times a coach will ask for information about the circumstances. This is not to find out about any problem but rather to provide a context from which to ask useful questions. When things are worse it can be for many reasons, some of which are outside the client's control and some of which might even be a 'side-effect' of progress. Having a sense of what sort of 'worse' it is helps the coach find the more pertinent questions.

When the situation is worse because the same difficulties faced earlier have increased, the most usual line of enquiry will be to find out why they are not even worse than they are. A client might have been drinking more although still doing a day's work

Coach: What are you doing to stop yourself drinking so much that you can't go into work?

Client: I can't not go into work – that would be the end of everything.

Coach: So what are you doing?

Client: Like I said, I can't let that happen!

Coach: I can see your motivation, *why* you stop yourself – but I'm also interested in *how* – what is it that you actually *do* that gets you to keep control of your drinking to this extent?

Client: I drink sparkling water. That can help.

Coach: And how do you decide to drink sparkling water instead of more alcohol?

Client: I remind myself of what I've got to lose; not just my job but my family and to say nothing of my self-respect. Not that I've got much of that left now.

Coach: And when you've reminded yourself, what do you then do that leads you to take control and drink fizzy water?

Client: I just make myself reach out – it's just there beside the other stuff.

Coach: How come? How come you have fizzy water on hand?

Client: When I go into one of these I always make sure it's there; it's the only thing that is going to save me.

Coach: So even before you begin you plan your exit strategy and make sure you have what you need to hand?

As the conversation develops the client discovers several other ways that he stops his drinking getting even worse than it has become. Later the coach asks what he would notice if his many existing strategies were simply to become a little more influential. What he could see was that it would actually be easier to begin implementing the stopping processes a little earlier in the sequence. As would be expected, as he noticed the extent of his active control drawing on that control seemed more feasible.

When the 'worse' is something outside the client's control then 'what's stopping it getting even worse!' is a less useful question. In an extreme situation the client's 'worse' might be that they have been made redundant although more usually it will be an organisational change that is creating potential difficulty. In these circumstances it is likely to be fruitful to examine the ways the client is coping with the stressful situation. It may turn out that from a personal point of view the client is doing exceptionally well. One client reported a redundancy after a long dispute (which had led to the initial referral). He was both pleased and surprised at how well he was dealing with what a few weeks earlier would have been a traumatic event. He put this down to a big rise in his self-esteem following the two previous coaching sessions and this had led him to review his role in the dispute. He realised he was justified for taking issue and although he lost his case he felt proud that he had stood his ground and was ready to get on with his life. It is worth remembering that the current of life will at times be with us and at other times against us. If the current is against a client we won't judge their progress so much by the distance they cover but will look at the strength of their swimming stroke. As (not only) the client made redundant said: 'I wouldn't wish what happened to me on anyone but I'm not sorry it has happened because now I know how strong I am – and how strong it's made me.'

Another version of 'worse' is when the consequences of improvement have unpleasant repercussions. A client said things were worse because the relationship between her and her business partner had deteriorated even further: 'I think I'd rather have him picking on me than this complete silence!' At first sight a coach might read this as a request to help get communication going again but by asking a few exploratory questions it was clear the issue was quite different. The client said the silence was because she had an argument with her partner that had gone badly wrong and that she 'deeply regretted', so much so that she was contemplating her resignation. In the previous session she had talked of her desire to become more assertive with her partner and to begin to make more of an impression on the firm's policy and direction. She had been determined to stand her ground more but had done so in 'the most stupid way': they had been travelling on the underground together to attend a meeting and she had objected to him holding her elbow to steer her into the carriage when the train arrived. Not only had she objected but had done so loudly and forcefully drawing attention to them both. Everyone had assumed her partner had made an unwanted sexual advance and he had 'felt humiliated' by it. They had not spoken in the 2 days since this event.

It was not long before client and coach were laughing. She had stood up to her partner, not in the cool sophisticated way that she had hoped but in the raw heat of a moment she felt his controlling behaviour went over the mark. Although no spoken words had passed between them written words had and on reflection these had been measurably more respectful than was usual. It was early days to know how it would end but as the client had moved in the direction she had hoped for it was likely that the outcome would be positive.

When asked how she would know this was the case she said she would not dread going to work so much, which it turned out was already beginning to happen. The next session was cancelled. The client and her partner had had a long conversation, sorted out some misunderstandings and were getting on even better than they had when they joined forces. Sometimes 'worse' is just a patch of rough ground on the way forward.

A summary of questions that might open up a fruitful conversation are:

- 'What things in your life have managed to stay OK even through such a bad period?'
- 'What have you been doing that has prevented it from being even worse?'
- 'What are the ways you have managed to cope with such difficulties during this time?'
- 'How have you managed to deal with such difficult situations before?'
- 'What do you think might be the first sign that you are getting back on track again?'
- 'Where, between zero and ten, would you rate your confidence of getting back on track?'
- 'What has prevented you from giving up even though things have been so bad?'

There are times when the client reports no change or an even worsening situation and whatever the coach asks seems fruitless. This is a time to check the contract by asking:

• 'What are your best hopes from this session?'

This is the question to ask every time a session runs out of steam or the coach has lost a sense of purpose or direction. This can happen if the coach has not quite managed to negotiate a clear enough contract or if the client's position has shifted somewhere along the way. This does not mean the question needs asking at every session but it certainly pays to keep it like a pocket compass just in case client or coach loses their way.

Closing the contract

Coaching does not have to be an ongoing process and until definite benefits can be demonstrated through research there is reason to see an ongoing contract as a 'perk' for those who enjoy it rather than a business tool that increases effectiveness. If an ongoing coaching contract is established then it may well be more effective if there is sufficient time between sessions for the client not to be able to rely on it for decision making or problem solving. Otherwise, the coach is likely to become 'part of' the situation she is working with and therefore less able to bring a different perspective. Imagine a senior manager who has found her first few coaching sessions really useful and begins to think 'that will be a good thing to take to my coach'. If the 'thing' is urgent this might mean a delay but if the outcome is a good one the delay is justifiable. The same thought might also apply to the more important decisions: 'I'll save that until my session'. There does not need to be much of this to create a dependency between coach and client with the result that the manager becomes less able to act independently and the coach inadvertently becomes a hidden (and therefore unaccountable) part of the organisation's decision-making process. When this happens the coach is likely to be costing the organisation significantly more than the coach's fee that they pay.

This creates a dilemma for coaches as much as it has for therapists. Longer contracts make for economic stability

and without a degree of stability many coaching organisations would have difficulty surviving. There is no simple
answer to this dilemma unless coaches are prepared to risk
offering more flexibility in return for greater effectiveness
and efficiency.

This is what the BRIEF approach offers: an issue-based
approach in which contracts are specific and come to an end
when the client decides. Where longer-term 'maintenance'
contracts are required these are infrequent, rarely more often
than 3 monthly and are geared towards review and forward-
thinking rather than specific issues saved for the occasion.
What this perspective leads to is a high incidence of single-
session coaching, a fair number of two-to-four sessions and
very few longer than that. To accommodate this more issue-
based approach coaching organisations would need to
organise themselves more like surgeries, being responsive to
need when it arises rather than when it is convenient, be
more likely to err on the side of doing less than more and be
more prepared to demonstrate their effectiveness through
outcome studies rather than marketing skills.

Issue-specific coaching

If the coaching contract relates to a specific issue as does
most of BRIEF's work the contract will end when the client
is as close as he decides he needs to be to the agreed outcome.
This might be something as broad as having 'more direction'
or as narrow as 'handling a specific meeting well'. When it
comes to deciding when to end the sessions the coach will
always trust the client's judgement. What criteria for ending
the sessions the client chooses will vary but it is usually
when enough of their preferred future is happening to justify
confidence in a lasting outcome. The specification of the
client's hopes therefore serves not only to generate their
occurrence but also provides an indicator of outcome. Very
often this realisation will occur between sessions and a
planned session might be cancelled. Similarly, an unplanned
session might be called for when the client finds they have
'terminated' too soon. Otherwise, the end will be realised
during the session in which the client is reporting events

close enough to the original description of a preferred future to make both client and coach question the need for further sessions. There is no great ritual for these meetings. Ideally the coach will not have become a majorly significant person in the client's life but simply a useful business associate whose acquaintance can be made and re-made as and if required.

Session-limited coaching

Some clients will want to commit to a set number of sessions and organisational constraints might require them to be at pre-specified intervals. Given the freedom, a solution focused coach will prefer to fix the times session by session, following the assumption that if things are improving it is more efficient to stretch the time between sessions. Following this practice a six-session coaching contract could easily stretch well over a year without any loss of effectiveness. However, whatever the preferences of the coach or evidence from outcome studies, the coach must where possible fit with the client's preferences and adjust to them accordingly.

If a fixed number of sessions is agreed and the client has a specific outcome in mind the coach might want to negotiate some flexibility. If the outcome is achieved in fewer sessions than have been contracted there would be good grounds to end there or at least 'bank' the remaining sessions for another purpose. To continue working towards an end that has already been reached is likely to be counterproductive as will be the 'invention' of an issue just to use up the resource.

Alternatively, the client might want to use the specified sessions for a more general purpose such as keeping focused, increasing job satisfaction or maintaining progress whereas others will decide to bring a specific issue on each occasion. In these cases the approach is likely to be similar to that adopted in a longer-term, open-ended contract.

Long-term contracts

Despite the solution focused coach's reservations that a long-term open-ended contract will produce diminishing returns or even get in the way of progress, some clients will still want a long-term regular commitment to coaching and on the principle that the 'customer is always right' the solution focused coach will need to find a way to adapt. The preference would be for widely spaced sessions that might tackle specific issues if any were convenient enough to arise at the scheduled time but otherwise the sessions would take the form of a backward–forward review. There are a number of trigger questions around which to build such a review.

- 'What have you been doing over the past 3 months that has helped you ... (keep on track/expand the company/ develop your team/given you the job satisfaction you want/ kept your work–life balance OK, etc.)?'
- 'What will you/your colleagues/your family be noticing about you over the next 3 months that tells you/them that you are ... (keeping on track/etc.)?'
- 'On a zero to ten scale how would you rate the way you are keeping on track (maintaining job satisfaction, etc.)?'
- 'And how would your colleagues/family rate you on the same scale?'
- 'If over the next 3 months you find you have gone up one point on the scale what might you/your colleagues/your family be noticing?'

All these questions would be openings to the conversations about fine detail that have been described in the previous chapters.

The coaching relationship

The coaching relationship is simply a business relationship. People are getting together to do mutually rewarding business. Like any other business relationship it requires whatever degree of trust is pertinent to the job in hand. The relationship between a company and its postal service requires sufficient trust for the postal service to know it will be paid and for the company to know documents will be delivered and not read or disseminated in transit. Not much thought needs to go into this level of trust. A lot more will go into a decision about choosing external accountants who will obtain some of an organisation's most confidential and sensitive information. And yet it is still a business relationship. Coaches will need to be trusted not to pass on information in the same way as any other associate. There is nothing special about this.

This view of the relationship will not sit well with a coaching style that seeks a long-term client–coach association in which coach and client have some 'special' relationship that somehow carries an import beyond all other business contacts. Although coaches do not always welcome comparison with therapists this sort of relationship is a clear reflection of those long-term therapy relationships whose usefulness is now seriously questioned. The solution focused coach would rather be invisible than significant; someone who generates and manages a conversation in which the client hears his or her own words either for the first time or with fresh ears. The end result should be that clients experience themselves charting and treading their own path unaided.

This preference for invisibility also reflects the dominant direction of trust in solution focused coaching: that is, for the coach to trust the client rather than the client to exalt the coach to a special status of trust. Giving such status to the coach is to fall into one of the traps laid by traditional therapists in which it is the client's job to trust the therapist (so they can bare their souls) and the therapist's responsibility to guard that trust. In solution focused coaching there is no need for soul-baring or any admission of weakness or fault. It is not asked for by the coach nor necessary for the coach to work effectively. The client is free to give or withhold whatever information they choose. The last thing the coach wants is the client to leave a session regretting what they have said. Instead, the coach will trust the client to guide them by their responses while the client can decide question by question whether or not to trust the coach. With this concept, trust is seen not as an accumulated commodity but as a moment by moment assessment of the relationship and its value to the client. Hence, in one of the earlier examples, when a client thinks a question is seeking to uncover a problem (between him and the team he manages) he withdraws his cooperation (and trust). As soon as he realises that this is not the purpose of the question trust (cooperation) is renewed. Trust, like cooperation, is seen as a process rather than a commodity.

An example of trust being withdrawn was provided by a client worried about the effects of his divorce on performance at work. He was responding openly and with interest to questions about his hoped-for future behaviour in which his personal distress, although still felt, was no longer having a negative impact on work. He had described his journey to work in the 'new' future and the following extract begins with him describing what Jo his PA, in whom he had confided, would notice.

Client: I'd be more upbeat, more interested in what the day held.

Coach: How might that show?

Client: Well I wouldn't just slump down and wait for my coffee! I might even make one for her.

Coach: What difference would that make?

Client: To her or to me?

Coach: Either, both.

Client: A big difference. She'd be relieved for a start. She's been marvellous but I know it's been a strain for her. And I'd be relieved.

Coach: What difference will that make to your conversation?

Client: We'll get on with the business sooner – and I'd be the one to initiate it rather than moaning when she did.

Coach: And then?

Client: I'd be able to go into the main office without having to steel myself.

Coach: What would you do instead – instead of steeling yourself?

Client: I'd look forward to working out the day with them.

Coach: Who'd be the first to notice that you were walking into the room looking forward to working out the day with them?

Client: Nobody. I don't let any of this get to them.

Coach: If someone did notice a difference what might it be?

Client: No they wouldn't. I've been very careful not to let this spill over. They rely on me to take a strong lead.

> And I'm very good at hiding my feelings. Jo's the only one who knows and even she doesn't know the half of what's been going on.

Coach: So how have you managed to do that, to keep up such a strong front even when things have been so bad?

Client: There's not much choice really. This isn't the sort of place you can show weakness. It's not that people are callous or anything like that – it's just that if one person lets things go it affects everyone, brings the whole show to a stop so you have to keep going whatever. I certainly couldn't afford to lose my job on top of everything else!

Coach: So how have you done it – how did you get yourself to keep going in the face of such adversity?

As soon as the coach asked who in the general office would notice the change the client's tone changed from one of thoughtful interest to clipped certainty. Though the coach tried once more it was clear that a 'no-go' area had been reached. The coach judged that he had asked an 'unsafe' question, that is, a question that the client saw as opening up the possibility of criticism and the suggestion that his personal problems were affecting the performance of his team. Rather than probe into this the coach adjusts his 'fit' and seeks to endorse the client's view by asking him how he did it. After exploring this successful struggle the client returns to the description of a better tomorrow.

Client: So what will you notice about yourself as you go into the main office not only looking forward to being with your team but also knowing you had successfully managed a very difficult period?

Coach: I'd have a sense of pride, not just in myself but in them, too. They're a good team!

Client: And how might they know that you felt this pride in them?

Coach: I'd probably make a point of looking for something favourable to say.

Client: Such as?

Coach: I don't know. Maybe I'd even thank them for putting up with my long face for so long. I know they must've noticed however much I try to hide it and really they've been very supportive and got on with things under their own steam.

This switch is typical of solution focused coaching conversations in which the client suddenly feels exposed to potential criticism, experiences the coach's shift to respect this privacy and then feels free to answer more openly when the question is put in a more fitting way.

A final word about the relationship between solution focused coach and client. In the above conversation, as in all the transcripts, it is possible to see how closely the coach follows the client's answers. This involves very concentrated listening and rapid decision making about which part of the client's answer to build upon. Being listened to (and listening) is one of the most humanising experiences available to us: more than anything else it is the process by which we are defined by others and by ourselves. Our lasting and most treasured relationships are likely to be those in which we both hear and are heard. The solution focused conversation replicates this experience. What is different is that unlike the relationships of friendship and love it is a professional relationship built around a specific purpose. The relationship is not the purpose but merely a by-product of the conversation it is necessary to hold.

Summary

- Each follow-up session in solution focused coaching is likely to start with a focus on what has been better.
- Even when the client responds by saying that there has been no improvement or that the situation has deteriorated this will not prevent the coach continuing to focus on what the client has been doing that has proven useful even in a difficult situation.
- Since most solution focused coaching is outcome specific the work will stop when the client has either achieved his

best hopes or is sufficiently close to feel confident that a good enough position can be reached and maintained.

- Endings do not typically require any 'working through' since the nature of the relationship minimises the likelihood either of dependency or of the coach being viewed as a central figure in the client's life. The solution focused coach will work to centralise the client and the client's perceptions rather than the coach and the coach's perceptions and thoughts.
- Ongoing coaching contracts, while rare, are constructed as a series of one-off meetings, each beginning with a review of the intervening period, focusing on what the client has been doing that he is pleased with, followed by a focus on how the client will know that the next intervening period will be a time of progress.

Activities: Follow-up sessions – 'What's better?'

On four or five occasions over 20 years one of the authors has been unable to attend a planned appointment and not been able to inform the client. On these occasions the client has been offered a session with another coach. Each time the new coach has begun 'blind' with the question 'What's better since your last meeting?' Clients have consistently reported that the ensuing session has been as useful and in no significant way different from previous ones.

These activities, which need at least two participants, are especially useful as a supervision tool where the person being interviewed takes the role of a current client who seems 'stuck'.

Activity 1: 'A lot better'

- Divide into coaches and clients. The 'client' needs only to give a name and age if the 'going blind' is to be replicated.
- It is a second or subsequent session.
- The coach (perhaps 'standing in' for another in order to make sense of having no prior knowledge) is to ask 'What's better?'

- The client is to answer 'Quite a lot actually'.
- (In giving the answer the client is referring to differences he has helped bring about rather than accidental or circumstantial improvements.)
- The coach is then to interview for at least 10 minutes concentrating solely on eliciting a description of the improvements, the client's actions associated with the improvements and the consequences of these improvements.

Variations

Activity 2: 'Not much'

The interview can be varied by the client answering 'Not much' and the coach repeating the search for those small improvements implied in the answer.

Activity 3: 'Things are the same'

In this version the coach might begin by exploring what the client is doing to stop things getting worse.

Activity 4: 'Things are worse'

There are many possible next questions. This activity is best used in order to try different responses in order to build a repertoire.

9

Back to work

This chapter is based on transcripts of three sessions adjusted to preserve the anonymity and confidentiality of Bill, the client. Some of the inevitable 'social conversation' has been edited in order to shorten the transcript otherwise it is essentially accurate. These conversations do not make a gripping read. They focus on the mundane and apparently obvious aspects of life, the small seemingly insignificant steps repeated day by day. To a reader they might even be soporific. To the client, however, they are quietly revelatory, while to the coach they are acts of craftsmanship, each question seeking out another facet of possibility.

The first session

Bill has been referred by his occupational health department. After a few pleasantries the coach gets down to business.

Coach: So what are your best hopes from coming here?
Bill: Well, as I think you know I'm off work with depression and unless I get back soon I'm going to lose my job so in the short term I'd hope to get back to work and to get some sort of framework to deal with this. In the medium to long term I'd hope next time I begin to feel down to be better prepared and less thrown off track.
Coach: OK.

Bill: Ups and downs have been happening all my life and I'd like to be better able to manage them better.

Coach: OK . . . so if as a result of our talking you got yourself back to work and then developed a way of thinking that made managing the feeling down times easier in the future that would make this worthwhile?

Bill: Yes.

Coach: And if you were to wake up tomorrow realising that you were ready to go back to work – not that you'd gone – but that you were ready – what would be the indicators, the signs to you that you were ready to go back to work?

Bill: That I could – I think it would be about having some more energy – being able to get out of bed and think I can go on with today – not feeling so sluggish – it would be about being able to concentrate again. I have to be able to concentrate for work because my work involves prolonged periods of concentrating. If I can't do that then I can't do my job.

Coach: OK so you need to be able to do that, to concentrate. What else would be a marker to you that you were pretty well ready to go back?

Bill: I'm not sure. I think it would be about not feeling anxious about it. Thinking that it will be good to go back rather than thinking 'I don't want to go back' and thinking about all the emails and the pile of phone calls and letters and irate people because I've been away.

Coach: Yes. So that would be a sign.

Bill: Yes – It'd be having the sense 'I can cope with that' and deal with those people and having the confidence.

Coach: So if you were feeling that bit more 'I can do this' . . .

Bill: Yes some sort of confidence.

Coach: OK confidence – so that'd be a good indicator too. Right – more energy, concentration, the confidence that I can do this and deal with the extra difficulty that going back to work always entails.

Bill: Yes.

Coach: So how would this energy be showing itself?

Bill: I'm not sleeping very well at the moment so – I'm waking up but not feeling that I can get up and do – I'm tired and lethargic – so waking up and feeling refreshed – not feeling sluggish.

Coach: I can imagine that that would make a difference.

Bill: Having had a good's night's sleep, feeling refreshed.

Coach: What other differences would this energy make if you were ready to go back to work?

Bill: I think it would be about getting things done you know.

Coach: Like what?

Bill: Doing the ironing, doing the washing, washing the dishes.

Coach: Basic everyday . . .

Bill: Basic housekeeping things that tend to pile up.

Coach: So on the day you realise you're ready, you'd be getting the day to day . . .

Bill: Yes because in my normal life that fits in – so if I cleared the backlog of that – so I'd go back to work knowing that I had the socks to last me the next week – those very practical things.

Coach: So having life in a shape that makes work possible – or easier. And who would be the first person to notice that you had your energy back and were ready to go back to work?

Bill: Probably a couple of my friends. Hannah probably.

Coach: How would Hannah know? What differences might she see?

Bill: I think it would be about actually engaging in conversations having some sort of spirit – at the moment I'm a bit wrung out because I don't have the – the conversation tends to drag – I don't have the spark.

Coach: So some of that would be back – that spark, that liveliness. How else would she know?

Bill: I'd probably be looking better.

Coach: In what way.

Bill: I think it would be about sort of – I'm not sure – having more energy and being more animated.

Coach: How would she respond?

Bill: She'd just show it.

Coach: Who else would be glad to see you getting back into your life?

Bill: Robert, another friend.

Coach: What would Robert be seeing?

Bill: Well again because I've known him for a long time – he's seen me through the ups and the downs, so the life that I'd be describing would be much fuller – I'd be talking about doing things, about going out, what else I was doing.

Coach: OK, so going out, seeing people, doing things – what sort of things would he be hearing you describe yourself doing if life was going well.

Bill: Going to the theatre, the opera, night classes . . .

Coach: So those sorts of things would be coming alive in your life again – that's clear – that's OK. So friends would be noticing – who else would notice that things were back on track in a good way?

Bill: I suppose friends at work would notice – just getting back to work really – they'd see.

Coach: Alright – OK if this were a change that happened little by little what would be the first tiny signs that would tell you that you were on the right track, that things were going right for you?

Bill: It'd be the sleeping and waking, there'd be a structure of going to bed and sleeping because at the moment when I'm not sleeping well – I'm sleeping in the afternoon – those cycles.

Coach: OK so those cycles they'd be re-established – so what else would be a sign that life was just beginning to move in the right direction?

Bill: I haven't been able to read except rubbish so if I could start reading again – pick up a book and look forward to reading it would be different.

Coach: OK so if you picked it up and said 'I want to read this' that would be a sign – just picking it up and wanting to read – OK. OK. *(pause)* Well, here's a very simple scale of zero to ten where ten stands for the day when you wake up when you just know that you're ready to go back to work and zero stands for the worst you've ever been, where would you see things now between zero and ten?

Bill: Probably five or six.

Coach: OK. That's a long way to have come. How have you done that?

Bill: Partly I think the prospect of coming here. I didn't want to come when they suggested it, to be honest it's not my kind of thing, but then I thought I'd better go along with it – didn't want to upset them.

Coach: A hard decision then.

Bill: Yes – if I hadn't had to do it, I probably wouldn't have – if I had a private income . . .

Coach: So how did you do that? To make yourself come rather than just ringing and cancelling?

Bill: I did think about that but I don't like to break agreements and I thought maybe it's worth a try – maybe speed up the cycle.

Coach: Hard to get yourself to do it?

Bill: Yes – it was. If I'd won the lottery I wouldn't have done it.

Coach: So since then, since you decided to come, what differences have there been?

Bill: I think it . . . I've been more willing to get out and to see people . . .

Coach: So you've been out to see people?

Bill: A friend from work – arranged to meet the other evening to have a chat. I don't feel that I was at my best but . . .

Coach: . . . you handled it in some way?

Bill: Yes not that it was difficult. She's known me so she understands and makes allowances.

Coach: OK so you've made yourself go out subsequently – What else?

Bill: I'm feeling that one of the things – getting the structure – is happening.

Coach: So is that another sign – getting some of the structure back?

Bill: Yes talking with people – being willing to take the

	phone call, to make the phone call, rather than letting the answerphone take it.
Coach:	So you've noticed that too. At this stage are you having to make yourself do it?
Bill:	Yeah, there's been a couple of times when the phone's rung and I've said 'no'.
Coach:	And other times you've made yourself pick it up?
Bill:	Yeah.
Coach:	So there's times you've made yourself do that – OK, so you're making yourself go out – you've re-established communication with the outside world – What difference do you think this is making?
Bill:	Because that's what my normal life is; taking pleasure in friends and life and if you're not talking to people you're not engaging with them – I'm not living the life that I want to live – I know that what I do is I hide – I stop communicating but I also know that that's not helpful.
Coach:	And what about in the house? What are the signs in the house while you are at home that you are at five or six?
Bill:	Making some use of the time even if it is just watching a DVD rather than just sitting – I have on occasions just sat and stared at the walls.
Coach:	Let's have another scale – ten you've got every confidence – let's just stick with the first thing that you said, getting back to work – ten stands for you've got every confidence that you will get back to work it is only a question of when you will do it – zero is the opposite – where do you see your confidence at the moment?
Bill:	Nine.
Coach:	Nine – pretty high.
Bill:	Because I've always got better – because I'm coming up I've passed the bit where – ones and twos – where I'm thinking 'am I going to?' I know life *is* worth living.
Coach:	Yes.

Bill: Yes, I am past the worst now.

Coach: OK so you know that – so it's only a question of time now? What else gives you confidence that you will come through this terrible time?

Bill: Just running through what I've done already has made me realise that I'm probably further along than I realised. I'm quite surprised really. Of the things that I think that I could do I'm doing most of them and of the ones I'm not doing I'm aware that I should be . . .

Coach: OK so you are already aware of other things that you could be doing. And when it was time to begin doing some of these other things how would you know?

Bill: I suppose in some ways it's already started. I know what I've got to do. It's just a question of finding the energy for another push. Yet I know that once I start doing more I will feel more energy. It's a bit of a chicken and egg – or catch-22!

Coach: Yes. Is that something that you have noticed in the past?

Bill: It is – it accelerates the more that I start doing things; it feeds back in to making other things possible.

Coach: So of the things that are hard to do that demand energy and in a curious way give energy, what are some of the things that you think that you might notice next?

Bill: I think that it will be the social getting out and meeting people and taking pleasure and not just very controlled on my terms – more 'we're going out to dinner do you want to come?'

Coach: OK so taking a step beyond that . . .

Bill: Yes just getting back in to the – hearing a joke – enjoying – getting back into the bonhommie –

Coach: Participating more fully in what is going on?

Bill: Yes.

Coach: And as you got you life back on track on this occasion what would be different that reassured you that

	you had more of a handle on it, more control, if you began to go downhill again?
Bill:	In the past things have dropped off and I've rationalised them until so many of them have dropped off that I realise that my life has changed shape – I think that by the time that I've started crying then I realise that for the last couple of months I've been letting myself go.
Coach:	Then you notice it . . . you turn back and notice it and think goodness . . .
Bill:	The reason that I didn't go to my night class was not just that I was too tired that day – the reason that I was too tired was part of a bigger picture.
Coach:	So if you had a way of noticing earlier – mmm – that might give you ways of not dropping so low . . .
Bill:	Yeah I hope . . .
Coach:	Sounds like it's tough doing things this way?
Bill:	Yeah it's not pleasant.
Coach:	Yes that's what I assumed. *(pause)* If you had to make a prediction now given where you see yourself – when would you be imagining that you'd be feeling ready to go back? Do you have a sense at the moment?
Bill:	If I take Christmas out of the picture – I'd say 2 or 3 weeks I would be thinking 'yeah I can do this'.
Coach:	So on the basis of your experience of this . . .
Bill:	Yes and I'm out and about and starting to . . .
Coach:	So this is a key sign for you?
Bill:	In the past – yes it's the hiding is the key thing that I'm aware of – when I'm not at my best I don't want to deal with the world, I want it to go away whereas if I can deal with the world even if it's on reduced terms it's starting to live a life again rather than having an existence.
Coach:	So both the going out and the taking the phone calls are evidences of that?
Bill:	Yes. Yes.
Coach:	What else are you noticing?
Bill:	It's being visible – it's being in contact – being in a social network, not being isolated and alone. I think

that it's probably planning and having some sense of future – having a mental connection – as an example reading is a very solitary activity – so sometimes you make mental notes 'I wonder if so and so's read this – next time I talk to them I'll ask'.

Coach: OK so even when you're on your own . . .

Bill: You're making mental notes and connections – 'I must lend them or I'm glad someone recommended this to me because I'm really enjoying it' – I'll have to tell them – So even sitting on my own there is a cast of virtual connections.

Coach: OK. I think that's my questions done – is there anything that I should have asked you and haven't asked you?

Bill: No.

Coach: Anything that you had in mind to say and you haven't had the opportunity to say?

Bill: No.

Coach: OK then let me just attempt a summary.

Bill: OK.

Coach: OK. I was just jotting down a few notes and what really struck me was your response to the scale question – ten standing for the day before you know that you are ready to go back to work and zero the opposite – you said that you were already between five and six – over half way and I was struck by that and by your very strong confidence that you would get back to work. You are already doing a lot and are also aware that there are a few things that you might find yourself doing that would just push that up a little bit further.

Bill: Yes. That seems fair.

Coach: I'd be really happy to talk some more with you if you'd like to come again?

Bill: Yes, that would be good.

Coach: How long a gap do you think?

Bill: What's the usual – it would be difficult for me to come every week.

Coach: Oh, that would probably be too soon, anyway. We usually err on the side of less rather than more so 2,

> 3, 4 weeks or even longer whatever seems enough
> time for today's discussion to make a difference.

Bill: Could we make it 4 weeks then?

Coach: Sure. Let's go down to the office and fix it.

This is a typical solution focused coaching session attending to the small detail of everyday life. There is no attempt to discover the cause of the problem and the only descriptions of it are unsolicited. Instead the coach concentrates first on Bill's hoped-for future – not the big picture but the first morning. As it becomes apparent that Bill is already improving, especially once this appointment was made, the coach moves to a focus on the past: firstly, the immediate past in order to specify each improvement and then a brief look at the more distant past in which Bill has built a track record of overcoming these episodes. The session ends with an encouraging summary but with no view from the coach about what Bill might do. It is assumed that Bill will have a sufficiently different perspective on his life as it is at this moment to promote new ideas about what he might do tomorrow. As so often in solution focused practice the focus is not on the journey's end but on the next small step towards that end.

Second session

The second session is 5 weeks later, just after Christmas.

Coach: So what's been better since we last spoke – it's been 4 or 5 weeks . . .

Bill: Well – I'm feeling a lot better – I'm back at work now.

Coach: Are you?

Bill: Yes, I went back on Wednesday, much sooner than I thought.

Coach: How did you know that you were ready to go back to work?

Bill: The barriers that I was aware of . . . the inability to concentrate, the lack of energy, all that was changing during the Christmas break – just more energetic – getting up . . .

Coach: OK, so more energy – I remember last time that that was important – that that seemed very central.

Bill: Yes.

Coach: You've seen that coming back over the break?

Bill: Yes, I've felt more relaxed – getting away and being in a different place has helped and when I came back that sense of more energy continued.

Coach: That continued. So how quickly did you realise that you were ready to go back to work?

Bill: It was pretty much on the Monday I thought yeah I'm feeling good.

Coach: So what led up to that?

Bill: It came down to a sense of every day I can continue – which I'd been feeling over the holiday. And just getting up over the holiday – even if it wasn't at 7 – meant that I was more tired at night and so I was getting a night's sleep.

Coach: And that again is different and . . .

Bill: Yes, I hadn't been sleeping well at all. The concern must be that being back at work the stress – or whatever it is – will get in the way of my sleeping and that is something that I'm aware of.

Coach: OK so you're aware of that . . .

Bill: Yeah and at work I've agreed with my boss just to work on one project while I catch up with things.

Coach: Is that helping?

Bill: In the past one of the problems that I've had is things getting beyond me – I usually try to juggle too many plates and it's keeping all the plates spinning all at once and that is something that in the past is something that I've found really difficult when you've got seventeen things and they are all important to someone else. So now, I've spoken with my boss, I'm being very clear what the restrictions are and I'm not taking on anything else at the moment and then we'll build up to a reasonable workload over the period of a few weeks.

Coach: And it sounds like your boss is sympathetic to this and sees the good reasons for doing things this way?

Bill: Yes absolutely.

Coach: So it sounds like this time you've thought that it is important to do some things differently?

Bill: Yes, that's come from various conversations.

Coach: So what else do you think that you're doing differently?

Bill: There are some things that I should be doing that I'm not doing – like taking breaks, but in terms of positive things I am leaving work behind at the end of the day – not taking piles of papers home although it is difficult to say yet that that has definitely changed since I am not really into work yet.

Coach: OK. And sounds like you are pleased with that?

Bill: Yes because it's about managing or failing to manage other people's demands, wanting to do everything and not having enough time so feeling that you can take things back and will get them done but of course you get home, watch some television, go to bed, get up and of course it's not done and then feeling bad about it rather than thinking that it is not done because I don't have the time instead.

Coach: So somehow managing your workload differently you think will help keep things on a more even keel?

Bill: Yes definitely – I have to talk to my boss about work-load management.

Coach: OK.

Bill: Not setting myself up with too much and then not getting things done.

Coach: Sure. It sounds like there's a question of balance there?

Bill: Yes. But at the moment it's just getting the boss to make the decisions about what's important.

Coach: OK, so it is going to be important to you to see your-self remaining aware of this issue? Keeping it alive?

Bill: Yes – my concern is if I get caught up – the same desk, the same job, and then the same ways of trying to manage it thinking that I can handle it all when I can't.

Coach: Not your responsibility at that level? OK. So this fits with the second issue that you raised and we will come back to that but in relation to the first issue, getting back to work, you've got through this quicker than ever before? And then the second issue – that when you're back you want to have confidence that you can keep things on track.

Bill: Yes.

Coach: So one of the things that you are going to need to see yourself doing to have confidence that you can keep things on track is being aware of workload, being aware of the boundary between home and work.

Bill: Yeah.

Coach: And recognising that some things just aren't your issue – what you are going to do and not do because you can't do it all.

Bill: Yeah.

Coach: So if we follow that track what else are you going to need to see yourself doing for you to feel that you're keeping things on track in a way that is good for you, in a way that allows you to be both productive and be happy?

Bill: Yes – knowing more clearly how to structure that – the happy bit not the work bit – I went to the cinema last night which was great – it didn't interfere with my life and it was nice to go out – it was that balance thing, making sure that those things happen. Not being so work focused, staying at work till half-past seven, taking work home but not doing it, feeling bad. So it's not just going home at six but it's having some tickets, doing something, arranging some-thing.

Coach: Yes.

Bill: Yes – buying the tickets means that it will happen. It was really nice.

Coach: Yes.

Bill: Being productive is about setting some boundaries, not letting the demands of other people or my desire to satisfy them lead me into taking on too much.

Coach: Yes.

Bill: Having a life and making sure that the life that I am protecting has some good stuff, has peaks in and making sure that there are as few troughs as possible.

Coach: So you'll want to see that continuing?

Bill: Yes.

Coach: So is that the sort of thing that it is easy for you to forget?

Bill: Yes.

Coach: OK so how do you remember – how do you find the balance?

Bill: Yeah I think that is the thing – it is the balance that is the goal, it's the making sure that it is still on the agenda – regularly – that's the thing that I'm concerned about because it is so easy to get caught up in other things.

Coach: OK so if you were to continue leaving your work at work what difference would that make to thinking about these things – to think about the things that you enjoy doing?

Bill: For one thing I'd know I had five clear evenings a week and it's easier to think about what I want to do with one of them but if I'm not sure about how much work I'll have to do then I can't make plans or you get a phone call and it's already 7 o' clock and you're still at work and it's too late and I can't be bothered to get up and go out – so if there were time boundaries as well as work boundaries then it would be much easier for me at 6 o' clock to think about what I'm going to do – I can do something if I want to.

Coach: And would you be pleased to see yourself doing that?

Bill: Yeah – I would quite like to do that but it would depend on how well I'm managing the demands of – sometimes if I've got a number of things unfinished sometimes it is easier just to stay a little longer to get them finished but then sometimes in the evening it takes an hour to do something that would only take 20 minutes in the morning when you are fresher the following day. So I'm aware that on the one hand if I could just stick to it it would be better but I'm also aware that there is a part of me that says 'I'll just finish this off'.

Coach: Are there times when it would be right to just finish things off and to stay? *(Since Bill seems unclear here the coach invites further clarification of his preferred future.)*

Bill: Sure – if something is needed for 9 the next morning I'm more likely to get it finished at 6 than at 8 the next morning and that may be a good reason for staying late.

Coach: Rather than just staying to get through the work.

Bill: Yes, rather than just doing the work – if it's the very first bit of a big piece of work then again just finish it but if I'm just half-way through . . .

Coach: So there are some good reasons and you'd need to stay aware of when you are doing this for good reasons and when it's just 'oh I'll carry on . . .'

Bill: Yes tied to the desk – yes there's lots of people working long hours just to be seen to be working long hours which is something that I've become aware of and in the past again there's been kudos to be there when the boss is leaving.

Coach: OK so . . . alright . . . so in relation to work there are a number of things that you are very aware of and it's going to be a question of acting on that awareness and keeping it alive?

Bill: Yes.

Coach: So let's imagine you are back into your routine, workload built up again, fully functioning *and* you are leaving it behind at the end of the day. As the afternoon wears on what would you be noticing different that fitted with arriving home, work-free and at a reasonable hour?

Bill: I think probably what I'm doing now – because I'm still very conscious of not overdoing it I'm planning my day more, so after lunch – and that's another thing, I'm making myself take a lunch break even if it's only 20 minutes or so – and after lunch I plan the afternoon more carefully so I know where I should be at 6 o'clock – not taken by surprise so to speak.

Coach: What difference does that make?

Bill: Mostly its good. Sometimes I get it wrong and try to do too much but usually I hit my target and as long as I've done that, even if the whole thing isn't finished, I'm OK about leaving. I don't so much feel the pressure.

Coach: It sounds like you are already building things into your future that could have quite a profound effect on your stability, on keeping your life going without so many ups and downs.

Bill: Yes and I'd also like to be spending my time in setting up a home, reading a book, listening to some music, and not having work-related things on the back of my mind and that goes back to the concentration thing and not reading the same page of the book four or five times because I'm thinking of something else. That'd be it because the boundary is not just space – work's not in my head, it's not at the forefront so that I can enjoy whatever it is that I am reading and get into it and the outcome of that'd be that I'm more relaxed and sleeping – and sleep is a thing that I'm still – if I'm relaxed and get to my bed at a reasonable hour and get a good night's sleep that'll also allow me to get to work and to be productive. So there's a hopeful positive sort of vision but obviously I'm still concerned about the things that could slide back.

Coach: What ways do you have of handling these intrusions?

Bill: I've never found a good way of doing that. What I've tended to do in the past is to go with it – to think that this is coming into my mind so I'll go with it for 10 minutes and come to a conclusion 'OK, what I am going to do is tomorrow morning I will do so and so and deal with this' and try to reassure whatever part of my brain is shouting about this – 'it's in hand, there's a plan'.

Coach: That sounds very practical – if you can't keep them out take them seriously, but not for too long.

Bill: I suppose it is in one way but I'd rather not have to do that. It seems a bit pointless just arguing with your own brain. I should be stronger about not taking work home.

Coach: What difference is it making at the moment as you are leaving work behind?

Bill: At the moment it's fine but I'm not really under any pressure. It's when I'm under pressure that I'm worried.

Coach: So one way or another a good sign would be you increasingly finding ways of concentrating on whatever it is that you are dealing with and not being refocused onto work during the evenings and at weekends?

Bill: Yeah – definitely.

Coach: So what difference does it make when you're with people – if you're with someone?

Bill: It happens less when I'm with people but I have in the past had a pen and paper in my pocket and when I've had flashes I've taken it out and made a note – they don't tend to play in the same way because there are more distractions so I tend to do the same thing of parking them.

Coach: OK so that's a parking mechanism – 'I'll just write that down'.

Bill: It's less common but happens from time to time.

Coach: What else is going to be a good sign that will tell you that this boundary is working well? What will you be doing with the space that – you'll be sleeping better or rather you'll be maintaining the improvements in your sleeping that you've already noticed.

Bill: I suppose I'll be doing those things in the evenings that I enjoy doing that I've sort of done less of or I'm not doing at the moment. One of the worries is about seeing time as a resource and trying to mine it – the 'work hard play hard ethos' is not one that I live well with. 'I've got some time I ought to be doing something with it'. Sometimes in the past I've just turned play in to work – it has become a pressure.

Coach: OK so being aware of that as well. So not working yourself quite so hard even in your own time.

Bill: Yes.

Coach: Just being aware of what works for you – you enjoy reading, listening to music, watching TV?

Bill: Yes doing things because I enjoy them – I realised that, a moment of revelation, not changing things that I do for pleasure into something that becomes like work.

Coach: Good. OK.

Bill: Goals have their place but milestones not millstones.

Coach: I like that – milestones not millstones. So that's something else that you'll want to see yourself bearing in mind. OK, so in terms of doing things differently what else do you think that you can learn from the past, the things that could be useful to you in the future in terms of establishing these habits that could be good for you?

Bill: I think it needs to be concrete – it's easy to say something vague. And then it does not have any impact it's too vague. It's 'what do I mean by a boundary?' 'And now it's 6 o'clock' that's a boundary. Drawing that line in the sand you know the thing about pleasure becoming work has to be made more concrete by saying that I'm not going to worry about achievement – when I do things I need to do them for the pleasure that I get out of them for the value that they bring me.

Coach: OK. Sounds like you've been doing a lot of reflecting?

Bill: As you say the issue is making it concrete and putting the habits in place.

Coach: By keeping doing it?

Bill: Yup – I guess. Actively, thinking about it, putting things in place, not just letting it happen by default.

Coach: An active thing – as you say. OK, on a scale with ten standing for 'you are back at work and you are as confident as you could be of maintaining that' and zero standing for the absolute opposite of that, where do you see yourself at present?

Bill: Probably eight.

Coach: OK. OK.

Bill: And that is because today is only day three back – if things go as they have been going then a week today I'll probably be at nine or ten. But at the moment I have to be a bit cautious – this is settling down, this is bedding in.

Coach: Sure.

Bill: But I'll take eight at the moment.

Coach: So what at the moment tells you that you're at eight?

Bill: My colleagues are very supportive, they've all been very glad to have me back – it's good to be back, it's nice to catch up with people's lives – it is a very positive atmosphere so that is helping me to feel positive. My boss has been very good about it and because I have been off for a shorter time I have come back to much less – less catching up.

Coach: So how long have you been off?

Bill: Just 6 weeks and that has included the holiday break.

Coach: Wow, that is considerably shorter than . . .

Bill: Yeah last time was 3 months and the longest that I have been off is way more than that.

Coach: So you've done this significantly quicker.

Bill: I do think that this has got something to do with becoming aware of trajectories and patterns and seeking to reflect – obviously if you do not go down so far you do not need to go up so far – that's the thing.

Coach: Gosh. So that is very significant. OK. And if there were three or four things you could notice that would reassure you that you were still on track what might they be?

Bill: Leaving work. Saying no and/or referring things to my boss for a decision. Leaving work at work and in so far as it is compatible with leaving work, finishing and letting go – yes, finishing things and putting them to one side.

Coach: And at home? What would be three or four things on the home side of your life that you would want to see yourself doing for you to remain as confident as you are now of keeping things on track?

Bill: The having regular peak out-of-the-house moments – whether that is dinner or whatever it is, using time at home to genuinely enjoy it rather than to perform to an invisible audience – stop performing and asking myself 'am I enjoying this?' Doing things for me – not for self-improvement – 'do I have to do this – do I want to read this?'

Coach: OK, what else? Those are two very clear and evident things.

Bill: I think being structured in some of the things that I do at home so that I can free up some of that time – there's something about if it's slightly structured then it takes up a certain amount of time and then it is done.

Coach: OK. So being more structured – getting it done. So is there anything else that I should have asked today?

Bill: No.

Coach: OK. Right. I'm very struck by the very significant changes since we spoke last and I can hear how useful to you the break was and it sounds as if you made every use of that time. I'm also struck by your very obvious thoughtfulness about this, which points to you wanting to put things in place in such a way that these sorts of troughs are less likely to happen in the future and I can hear that you are aware that reflection itself is not enough – that you have to do something? And then you have put these thoughts into action and are already noticing some of the benefits.

Bill: Yes.

Coach: So would it be useful to you for us to meet again? Maybe leaving it a bit longer than last time since you've made so much progress?

Bill: Yeah. Maybe make it in a couple of months; by then I will have some experience of the fight back as it were.

Coach: OK let's look at our diaries.

Third session

The whole of the third, and what proves to be the final session, is determined by the client's first answer: an unequivocal report of significant progress. As the session unfolds the client constantly refers to issues that have not yet been satisfactorily resolved. If it seemed that these snags and loose ends were standing in the way of progress the coach might have dealt with them differently, for example, by inviting descriptions of a future where the issue had been resolved or by exploring steps already taken. However, in Bill's case the loose ends are part of the effects of progress and to treat them as 'problems' to be solved is likely to slow that progress down. Another temptation would be to join Bill in his curiosity about the root of the problem. He is a reflective man and his thoughts about the problem seem to be helpful to him in working out a way forward. The coach confines himself to an interest in the positive effects of thoughtfulness rather than the thoughts themselves.

Although the session looks simple and straightforward the coach is taking a disciplined position, acknowledging and honouring each of Bill's answers while at the same time making careful choices about exactly which part of each answer to follow.

Coach: OK. What's better?

Bill: Um – I'm at work. I'm back on the writing course I started just before all this happened. I'm coping – mostly. I'm feeling pretty happy about leaving work behind when I leave.

Coach: You are?

Bill: I've taken no work home with me.

Coach: Wow. Over the last 2 months?

Bill: Yes. These are the positive things – there are others.

Coach: I'm sure there are! And how have you been doing that – taking no work home?

Bill: I'm just not doing it – I have had a conversation with my line manager. There is still some to-ing and fro-ing with both of us being unable to judge how long is a piece of string but in the sense of the negotiation of deadlines we're working that out.

Coach: So you've found a way of getting her on board?

Bill: Yes. To some extent – we're not there yet but I'm confident that we can get there – there's no reason why not – it is as important to her as it is to me that I don't go off again.

Coach: So what have you been doing that has been helping to get this sorted?

Bill: Being clear, being upfront, not feeling that I will have failed if I don't get everything done that people ask – handing over more of the responsibility to her rather than thinking that I have to deal with everything on my own.

Coach: Wow! That sounds like quite a change – how have you been doing all this?

Bill: Well, I have been keeping the idea of balance in mind and remembering how important it is not to get overwhelmed.

Coach: I guess that that's not been easy. How difficult has it been not to end up getting back into taking stuff home again? Have there been times when you've almost had to make yourself put the file down?

Bill: Yes it's been difficult for me. One of the other things that I was going to do was to leave on time – but I have been staying a little bit longer to get things done so I don't have to take it home. I don't mind that as long as it's just an hour and I'm not letting it drift too much.

Coach: Would you say that it has been most days of the week that you've been working late or some days?

Bill: Maybe once a week there'll be – I've got a post-it up which says 'go' but I'll want to finish it so I ignore it – something pops up so I'll get to the end.

Coach: What difference has this change made, mostly leaving on time and not taking work home?

Bill: It's felt very positive for me in the sense of my time, my personal time, it's felt slightly threatening at times in relation to delivering – it's been a reduction on what I used to do because I'm not used to working that way.

Coach: And yet somehow you've managed . . .

Bill: Maybe a lower work rate over the year may end up with the same productivity as a higher work rate over shorter bursts and then falling apart.

Coach: This sounds like really important changes that you're working on at the moment in the context of a working life.

Bill: Part of the reflection is that even if I got into bad habits – investing time in thinking – they're only habits, they are not tablets of stone – what am I getting from working until ridiculous hours – I'm not getting anything from it when I could be seeing friends.

Coach: Absolutely.

Bill: But the concern is still there about how effective the negotiation is because it is such a nebulous concept the work we do – it's not like spray painting – a lot of it, the research side is never really finished.

Coach: That's tricky negotiating this. I guess that you've already had some of these negotiations with your line manager?

Bill: Yes, about how for us both it's better to understand what is reasonable to be met.

Coach: So there's a negotiation about that?

Bill: Yes, trust – it's just about being very clear about what is achievable and not feeling that the boundaries and the guidelines are set in stone and if I choose to cross them it is because I choose to and not because something catastrophic is going to happen if I don't.

Coach: Sounds like a nice distinction – one that could be useful!

Bill: I don't want to create a rod for my own back but a nice balance of getting the work done, getting out of work early and having a life.

Coach: Yeah it sounds like you have had a little extra time even though sometimes you have stayed late. What have you done with the extra time that has been good for you? You said that you're back on your writing course?

Bill: Yes I have gone back. Maybe not the best week to mention it because it is this week that an assignment is due but I am enjoying it – it is intriguing and fascinating and it's been reassuring too – managing to concentrate, to get back into it and feeling able to focus.

Coach: That's great.

Bill: A new piece and then stop and put it to one side and on to the next.

Coach: So presumably some of your time has been going back in to the course. What else have you done with the extra time?

Bill: I've seen friends and family and a weekend away. I've done various social things as well as just spending some evenings sitting in and reading and I've managed not to have to feel that I have to be busy.

Coach: Sounds great – so it's OK to stay in and not have to do anything – being in is OK?

Bill: Yes whether that is working for my course or just to read. At the moment it feels balanced and it does not feel precariously balanced – you know the balance – stably balanced not on a knife edge ready to topple over.

Coach: It feels stable at the moment?

Bill: Yes flexibly stable.

Coach: OK, so some give and take – some flexibility?

Bill: Obviously there could be a crisis which would mean that I would have to work longer hours – I'd have to drop other things but there'd still be a sense of sustainability of living and enjoying the balance.

Coach: And you'd find a way back to something that was more sustainable – you'd have a sense that you could go back – I guess – OK?

Bill: Yes.

Coach: So who might have noticed the difference?

Bill: There've not been that many people who have noticed – Hannah from work – she has said I look more relaxed and happier.

Coach: Good – OK.

Bill: Without knowing where it has come from.

Coach: Good. Good. OK. Alright so it's your phrase 'boundaries and guidelines' we're not talking about staying rigidly on track – we're talking about a fluid and overall stable balance – stably balanced, not on a knife edge?

Bill: That's right.

Coach: So let's have another scale with ten standing for you being absolutely confident of maintaining this change even though you still have some uncertainties about your negotiations with your line manager and some stuff still to sort out and nought is the opposite of that – no chance at all – where do you see things right now?

Bill: An optimistic nine.

Coach: Wow!

Bill: Obviously – it's the external things – while things are as they are it is maintainable.

Coach: Great and it feels good to live your life this way?

Bill: Key things over the past 4 to 6 weeks have been 'what does it feel like when it is going right?' – this is not right, this is not long-term maintainable.

Coach: So you've got a sense now of what feels right to you?

Bill: Yes and that includes even how much rubbish TV I can watch and when to read something. I do think the more that I – there's still a bit more of getting that personal feedback of how things are when they are right and I still need to work on reflecting back 'is that a good balance' and that is part of the nine and not ten 'is there an external stressor'.

Coach: I like that – obviously it's difficult to have this 100%
           but you have much more of a sense of what it feels
           like to get things right for you – a position that you
           can hold and in future an experience with which
           you can compare other states – 'this isn't right, I
           need to do something about this' – that's great!

Bill: Obviously the proof of that pudding is in the eating
           when it comes to it.

Coach: Of course.

Bill: I could be fooling myself but at the moment I
           feel that the longer that it goes on and the more
           experience that I have of it . . .

Coach: And I guess the more experiences that you have of
           feeling it go one way and then nudging it back into
           balance – I guess those rebalancing experiences – it
           sounds as if those might be helpful to you. OK. So
           what will you be on the lookout for that tells you
           that you are staying on track with this?

Bill: I need to continue to reflect, not necessarily
           every day, on what's happening in maintaining
           the guideline positions and do those things – you
           know it's about creating the time to do the things
           which bring pleasure and joy into my life – you
           know actually do them – getting to see those films
           – you know reflecting on the benefits even if I am a
           bit tired.

Coach: Yes.

Bill: Maybe I was a bit tired but was it more than that –
           being morose – hiding – I'm so incredibly exhausted
           that I'm going to fall asleep – I don't think that I was.

Coach: So it's about challenging yourself sometimes?

Bill: Yeah – it's easy for me to talk about the external
           workload things – negotiate boundaries – manage
           time yet the more ephemeral – 'was that genuine?'
           'was I really that tired?' – the behavioural . . .

Coach: Habit . . .

Bill: Yes habit – yes the bad habits that I am trying to
           challenge in myself that's the . . .

Coach: So it sounds like now you are developing some
           better habits!

Bill: Yeah. You don't have to accept every invitation but you do have to be honest with yourself about the reasons why not.

Coach: And sometimes it sounds like you are saying that there might be some value in doing something even if you are feeling a bit tired – am I understanding that right?

Bill: It depends what you are doing and sometimes you can be energised by doing something that you did not feel like doing – I can't be bothered but 4 hours later it can turn out to be one of the best decisions that you have made to drag yourself out.

Coach: OK. So seeing yourself bring that level of awareness and reflection and a willingness to challenge your first responses – certain sorts of responses and thinking how genuine was that? Alright, that's clear. So what else might you notice that will be a sign to you that you are keeping things on track and keeping things going?

Bill: I think that it is having all those activities ongoing in a reasonable balance, reasonably up to date, there isn't too many days' worth of dishes – all concrete things are happening – it's one of the most important things to me because it's the most obvious and then things about personal, social engagement and I think obviously the negotiation of the work thing to deliver quality work within the boundaries negotiated – I do – I can't articulate any other clear things apart from those four or five key things happening within a reasonable balance; what I am doing and not doing.

Coach: Within a balance – within a range of OK positions?

Bill: Yeah.

Coach: And then you start seeing them just a little over this side or that?

Bill: And reflecting on that and thinking what is the counterbalance and thinking is that personal or external.

Coach: A lot of what you are talking about is about reflection and awareness and just taking the time to

> evaluate and review some of these things that you know in the past have been little signs that things have not been going quite as well and that would mean if you notice that you're beginning to lose energy catching it quicker.

Bill: Yes, yes.

Coach: Preventing the bigger dip – that sounds good.

Bill: One of the gaps I'm still thinking about is what is energy and what is energising because actually doing nothing seems to take up more energy than it saves!

Coach: OK, following that what is most energising in your life?

Bill: At the moment I'm finding seeing friends – you know that sort of relaxed informal time together even when I am tired and thinking why am I doing this – is most energising instead of isolating myself which compounds the loss of energy and becomes a vicious cycle.

Coach: OK, I can see that. So who's noticed, apart from Hannah?

Bill: I think my sis will notice a difference when I see her at the weekend.

Coach: What do think she'll see?

Bill: Much more perky – it'll be interesting to think about what they all notice and see if there is any unsolicited feedback about the changes in me that she's noticing then that will be confirmation that it is noticeable to people who have not seen me for a while.

Coach: Sure, OK, so keeping the balance and looking for evidence that you are getting your energies right?

Bill: An interesting thing just this weekend I was thinking that my course is coming to an end and in some ways that will be relief. But then I've also got my eye on another course and the question I asked myself is why I do this? Because I want to or because I feel that I ought to?

Coach: So once again, a growing thoughtfulness, weighing things up, working out what's right for you?

Bill: Exactly.

Coach: OK. We need to be stopping soon. How close do you think we are to finishing our work together – what are your thoughts on that?

Bill: Funnily enough I was asking myself the same question which surprised me a bit because on the way here I was thinking I'd need at least one more session but I'm not so sure now. Do you think I need some more?

Coach: To be honest I'd be inclined to trust your judgement on this though I would say that on balance less is probably better than more. But it's up to you and how confident you are in staying on track.

Bill: I am confident so let's leave it here. I can always get back to you if things go pear-shaped.

Coach: Of course you can. And I think you have good grounds for feeling confident.

Of the four contracted sessions only three are needed and Bill returned to work after the first – a significant change to a long-term pattern. The solution focused coach will rely as much as possible on the client to know when to stop meeting and had Bill decided, as many clients do, that getting back to work was enough and cancelled the second session then the coach would have supported this decision. For many clients just getting things moving again is all that is necessary while others will prefer to keep company for a little longer.

Activities: At your best

A key skill in solution focused coaching is to elicit descriptions of minutiae. An 'all purpose' starting point for an aspirational description is to ask a client to imagine him or herself 'to be at your best', for example 'on your next day at work'. Remember, this is only the client being at his or her best; neither the world nor the weather will be affected.

Activity 1: Lists

- This activity can be easily done alone although like all coaching activities if performed as a conversation it is likely to be even more effective.
- Imagine that it is your next day at work and you are at your best.
- List ten things (specific and observable) you will notice about yourself in the first 5 minutes after entering the building that will fit with you being at your best.
- List ten things (even more specific and observable) that your colleagues will notice about you in the second 5 minutes after entering the building.
- List ten things you'll notice about yourself as you leave work that will fit with you still being at your best.

Activity 2: Narrative

This will work best as a practice coaching session but instead of lists the coach seeks out a second-by-second sequential description of the person from the moment of entering the building, coming through reception, standing in the lift, passing colleagues in corridors, entering offices (or whatever this journey entails). The description should include the client's self-perception, what each other person (e.g. security, reception, strangers and known people in the lift etc.) might observe and what interactions might take place between them.

A 10-minute interview should not get beyond the first 15 minutes of the working day.

The effect of these detailed interviews, especially in relation to challenging days, can be dramatic.

10

The manager–coach

All the skills described so far can be used by managers as well as coaches. That part of a manager's job which is to do with enabling performance and the professional development of staff will benefit greatly from the application of solution focused skills. At the same time there is a very significant difference between the two roles, coach and manager. A coach is commissioned by and accountable to his clients. The coach works to the client's agenda and goals and if the client is dissatisfied the contract with the coach can be terminated. The relationship between manager and worker is the opposite: the worker must work to the manager's agenda and goals and if the manager is dissatisfied the worker can be dismissed.

In complex organisations no distinctions are absolute and the roles of coach and manager necessarily overlap. A manager will at times get better results by consulting and negotiating with staff and at other times straightforward instruction might work best. How each manager balances the enabling and supervisory will differ but for the balancing act to work the authority and responsibility of the manager must be clear.

The manager is required to ensure that:

- the purpose and goals of the organisation are being worked towards at all times;
- staff have the required competence to complete the tasks expected of them;
- staff complete to the required standard the work expected of them;

- where staff need to collaborate they do so in the most effective way.

These functions cannot be carried out without some form of inspection and monitoring by managers and where there is a shortfall in performance the manager must take remedial action. At one end of the spectrum this might mean extra coaching for a member of staff and at the other end it could mean someone being dismissed.

However, the position of the manager–coach is different. The manager is not disinterested in the way that the coach must be; disinterested that is in the specifics of the direction chosen by the client. The manager has a legitimate stake in how each team member is performing, in the choices that are being made about what work to prioritise and how to carry out that work most effectively. The manager's view will also be fundamental to the likelihood of promotion or disciplinary proceedings and dismissal. The manager cannot step away from the work in quite the same way that the independent or 'disinterested' coach can. Nor can those reporting to the manager expect the same level of openness to whatever direction they choose to move and whatever they choose to focus on in their 'coaching'. The manager must always bear in mind the interests and purposes of the organisation because she will be the one held accountable for the organisation's performance in her sector.

Much of the time, however, this difference can be safely and properly ignored, notably when the interests of the manager and the interests of the staff member can be seen to coincide. In these circumstances the manager–coach can treat the work as if the coaching commission emanates from the 'client', a client who just happens, in this instance, to be a member of the manager's team. As often as not both the manager and the 'client' will be equally committed to the 'client's' professional development because the 'client's' development will involve enhanced performance and that is likely to be good for both the individual and the organisation. Similarly both are likely to be interested in the 'client' finding a way through a stressful situation, a way that has to be both good for the 'client' *and* good for the organisation.

Both might be interested, when, for instance, the 'client' returns from a period of sick leave due to stress, to find a way of working that allows the 'client' to give of his best, in a way that meets both his needs and those of the organisation, in so doing reducing the likelihood of further periods of sick leave. At a time when the worker–client takes on a new responsibility, worker and manager, client and coach, will both be interested in cooperating to ensure that this new challenge is successfully faced. In circumstances such as these the manager–coach can draw on the solution focused approach in a manner that would be hard to differentiate from an external coach coming in to an organisation and providing 'disinterested' coaching to staff.

However straightforward the application in this context might be, that does not mean that it will be easy for the manager–coach and perhaps the greatest challenge to the manager will be to shelve, for the moment at least, her own certainty, her own knowledge often based on her substantial experience of working in the organisation, of the *correct and best way* to move forward. This is easier said than done. As soon as we become convinced that we know the 'right' way, it becomes almost impossible to be genuinely curious in the way that the solution focused process requires, genuinely curious, that is, to establish the 'client'/team member's *own best way* to move the situation forward, which of course only the team member herself can determine. As Adam Kahane (2004: 53) writes in his book, *Solving Tough Problems,* an account of the work that preceded the political changes in South Africa leading to the peaceful acceptance of the African National Congress (ANC) as a political player, 'Being an expert is a severe impediment to listening and learning'. So the effective manager–coach will always be attempting to notice those times when her own delusions of certainty are getting in the way of uncovering the alternative expertise of the worker–client, and in so doing, developing a stance of genuine openness, may indeed learn about new and potentially even more effective ways of managing the team's task.

It is precisely this that the most talented managers consistently achieve: subordinating any need on their own part to be 'the one who knows' to the developmental needs of their staff, and regularly finding space to invest their curiosity and energy in supporting each worker in developing his or her own competence through thoughtful reflection. Letting go of our own sense of rightness, of our illusion of certainty that we have access to the best way, maybe to the only way (as we might see it) and this represents an act of disciplined will on the part of the manager. This does not happen by chance but emerges from a chosen stance, from a belief that, in the long term, it saves times to work with team members to develop their independent competence, rather than to foster their respectful, deferent, dependence. So the team member who comes to her manager concerned about a meeting that she will be chairing and leading the next day with the request 'give me some tips' might be met with the response 'Sure I can but I'd like just to get a sense of your best way of doing this first?' The manager is not devaluing or withholding her own knowledge but recognises that her colleague will probably do best by working from the basis of her own skills. The manager will also be able to impart her knowledge through the questions she asks. For example:

Manager–coach: How might you respond if you feel your authority is being challenged?
Worker–client: I'd just ignore it and carry on.
Manager–coach: And if the challenge continued, was even taken up by others?
Worker–client: I suppose I'd have to deal with it.
Manager–coach: And if you were at your best how might you notice yourself doing that?

In this interchange the manager is asking a question based on her experience of what is likely to happen, her team member offers one way to deal with a situation that the manager's own knowledge makes her think might not be enough and this knowledge helps create the next question, which is still aimed at bringing out her colleague's own expertise. Ideally, this process should continue until enough shared knowledge has been identified to make the meeting a likely success.

Determining the agenda for change

However, the more challenging situation for the manager–coach will be working with those situations where the perspectives of the individual and those of the organisation are not so obviously coinciding.

In the following example a team member has been under-performing, failing to respond to affirmative support and to the training opportunities that have been offered. Since his last appraisal there has been a deterioration in performance with deadlines and targets increasingly missed and ignored. The team member has at no time voiced his own concerns but recently has been avoiding contact with his manager. Having attempted a purely collaborative approach and seen no positive results the manager adopted a more overtly challenging position, laying the concerns of the organisation and the predicted consequences of 'no change' clearly before the employee and inviting engagement in a change process. It is now the manager who is setting out the agenda for change in the context of competency proceedings, specifying what is required. Fortunately, this does not make the manager's solution focused skills redundant. The staff member, albeit reluctantly, bought into the requirements for change so enabling the manager to resume a more solution focused style.

Manager–coach: You need to know exactly where you stand and what we need to see from you to turn things around. Can I just set the position out so that you are quite clear?

Worker: OK.

Manager–coach: I will put this in writing to you for both of us to be completely clear about what is expected – but in summary there are four things that I need to see. I need to see you hitting your deadlines for your routine reports, I need to see you meeting your targets by the end of this quarter, I need to be convinced that you are fulfilling your contract in terms of your hours of work and that you are actually working during those hours and finally that you

	are contributing to the team in terms of developing our procedures and practices. Overall I need to see you pulling your weight in this team. Is that a fair summary?
Worker:	Yes.
Manager–coach:	OK. Well, is this something that you want to work on with me – turning things around?
Worker:	Yeah, I guess. I don't have much choice, do I?
Manager–coach:	Well you do! And I just want you know what the consequences are likely to be for you if I am not seeing change.
Worker:	Sure and I'd rather stay on and work something out.
Manager–coach:	Then let's get going. Imagine that tomorrow you come into work and you are on track towards fulfilling the department's expectations of you – what is the first thing that you will notice that will tell you that you are on track?
Worker:	Well it would help if people were friendlier to me when I come in.
Manager–coach:	What would be the first sign of them being friendlier?
Worker:	They might say hello – I'd feel more included in things.
Manager–coach:	What difference do you think that might make to your day?
Worker:	I'd feel more accepted, more a part of things.
Manager–coach:	What difference might that make?
Worker:	I'd want to contribute more – I'd feel more motivated to get on with things.
Manager–coach:	And if you were contributing more, getting on with things, what difference might that make to the rest of the team?
Worker:	They'd probably talk to me more, be more accepting.

It is not uncommon when someone feels criticised to locate the 'cause' for the difficulty externally. In future focused conversation this 'cause' is likely to be translated into a desire, in this case for a better relationship with colleagues. The coach goes with the constructive 'desire' rather than the implied blame and so is able to help the colleague begin to generate a realistic picture of better working relationships.

There are two key points for the manager–coach to keep in mind. The first is that however much the worker may state that he wants things to change, the manager will still have to be convinced that the changes are indeed happening and therefore alongside the 'coach's' stance of curiosity and interest, watching out for progress, there will need to be a parallel monitoring that the specified expectations are indeed being met. This is the added complexity that inevitably makes the position of the solution focused manager–coach more challenging, not just being sensitive to signs of progress but twin-tracking that interest with performance monitoring, a checking stance that is informed by a quite difference ethos from the more appreciative stance of a purely solution focused approach.

The second challenge to the manager is to be clear about the required outcomes but not about the means by which they are to be achieved. In situations where we become anxious, particularly if our own reputation may be at risk, then the tendency is to reduce uncertainty by outlining exactly what the worker must do and exactly how they must achieve their targets rather than just outlining the targets and working with the worker's own best ways of achieving those targets. Indeed the more anxious we are the more controlling we can become and paradoxically the more we can jeopardise the likelihood of a successful outcome. Specifying how targets must be achieved is often experienced by workers as overcontrolling of them, micro-managing, in a way that can lead to allegations of bullying and to a refusal to cooperate. When not only the target but the path towards it are specified then the only scope for freedom of expression that the worker is left with is to find ways, however subtle, to refuse to cooperate. This inevitably risks leading to the opposite of what the manager was attempting to achieve, namely a higher level of guarantee that the worker will perform as expected. In the case above the manager might well have ideas, based on experience, of the best way to meet deadlines but these are unlikely to match exactly those of the colleague. Rather than imposing, or even proposing these ideas the manager might ask questions like 'What will you/your colleagues/I notice that fits with you working successfully towards your deadlines?' These would be the signs to look out for and possibly comment on when seen while at the same time fulfilling the managerial responsibility of checking that the deadlines are actually met.

Binney and Williams (1995) in *Leaning into the Future* refer to a similar process that they name *freedom within a framework*. The framework is specified by the manager who sets out expectations and requirements, while the freedom that is to be explored resides in the worker's own best way of achieving these expectations and requirements. As the manager invites the worker to imagine what he will notice about himself and the way that he is approaching his work on a day that he is performing to his potential, the manager is holding open the freedom for the worker to discover his own best way of making progress. The trust that is implicit in this position is likely to strengthen the manager–worker alliance, to allow the worker to own the potential solutions discovered and thus be more committed to the success of the project. For the manager this trust is offered conditionally since it can only continue to be extended to the worker while there is sufficient evidence of progress at a sufficient pace to meet the legitimate needs of the organisation. At first this might seem a one-sided bargain – do as you are told or else! What makes it a genuine contract of more than just labour for money is the solution focused manager's real interest in the hopes and aspirations of his staff. The contract is still with the individual as it would be with an independent coach and the way forward is still the 'client's' but taken within the requirements of the team and the organisation. A common starting question might then be 'Let's imagine you come into work tomorrow and can get on in a way that is absolutely right for you, right for the team and right for the organisation; what is the first thing you'll notice about yourself as you are coming through the door?'

This is, in fact, the equation for all members of all organisations that are successful over time. Where such a synergy does not exist energies will be misdirected, at best wasted and indeed potentially destructive. However, such collaborative working relationships require constant attention from managers, looking for and appreciating achievements, checking levels of job satisfaction and always being interested in the expertise of those doing the job. Without this attention the default position of hierarchy, power and inevitable 'resistance' is likely to prevail. Allan Wade (1997) from Canada who has worked extensively in the field of oppression, whether in the form of childhood abuse or indeed political oppression states that people always resist oppression. In organisations where the livelihood of the worker is normally dependent on continuing employment that resistance will often take the form of disengagement, albeit disguised, from work and from the aims and goals of the employer. In a study carried out in 2002 by the Gallup Organisation and cited by Secretan (2004) 55% of employees were regarded as 'disengaged' with a further 17% deemed to be 'actively disengaged'. This is not to say that a solution focused approach will always work. If the job continues to be poorly done a manager might have little option but to micro-manage, if only to gain sufficient evidence for demotion or dismissal. Staff know that this power exists and can be used 'against' them hence the need for constant evidence that their managers are genuinely and always seeking a win–win outcome: good for the individual and good for the organisation.

Conflict resolution

Conflicts between team members, between teams or between managers and their staff are associated with a major drain of organisational energy, a reduction in creativity, a flurry of grievances and a potential for significantly higher levels of staff turnover. All of these side-effects are enormously costly and within smaller teams and organisations can put into jeopardy their very survival. The potential that solution focus holds in the arena of conflict resolution should be clear. Any approach that attempts to explore the past, to focus on what the participants have been doing that is wrong, that attempts to assign fault is clearly likely to exacerbate the blaming processes that are already associated with the stuckness that is being experienced. As a Belfast taxi-driver, a man well versed in the realities of enduring conflict knew only too well, the possibility of lasting change following the Good Friday agreement depended on the capacity of all parties to the conflict being able to 'keep looking forward'. In such circumstances solution focus is an ideal model although there are a number of factors to be borne in mind.

In any situation of determined conflict it is virtually unknown for either or any of the participants to believe that the onus of change lies with them. If this were to be the case the conflict would be long resolved. Thus, it is almost always the case that each or all of the participants take the view that it is the other or others who should make the first move. This can be voiced in many ways but often takes the form, expressed one way or another, 'I just want to hear him say that he is sorry for what he did. An apology – just that!' If the manager–coach's response to this is on the lines of 'look, neither of you accept that you are in the wrong and surely now is the time to move on and to look forward', however reasonable that can sound to someone not engaged in the conflict, to the aggrieved team member it can sound as if the manager is refusing to accept his 'innocence' and worse than that may be covertly allied to the other party. This risks leading to an increase in complaint that is intended to 'prove' that the other is the guilty party and should be punished. The almost inevitable increase in 'problem-talk' is only likely to make the already stuck situation more stuck as all the participants rehearse, over and over, their own reasons for being right.

Thus, instead of challenging the team member's frame the solution focused manager–coach will attempt, as far as is possible, to cooperate with the team member's account, working closer to the team member's position where more flexibility is likely to be found. Thus the team member who requires an apology can be asked:

Manager–coach: So if he were to apologise it sounds like that would make a big difference to you.

Worker:	Of course it would – I've been waiting for him to accept that he was in the wrong about this and should not have said what he said in public.
Manager–coach:	So how would he know that you were pleased that he had taken this step, what would he notice different about you?
Worker:	I suppose that things would go back to more like the way that they were before this whole episode.
Manager–coach:	So if they did – if they went back to more like the way that they were before this episode – what would he notice different about you?
Worker:	Well, we have hardly said a word to each other for months now.
Manager–coach:	So what would he notice different that would tell him that things were pretty much back to the way that they were?
Worker:	More talking, more support maybe, more interest in his projects.
Manager–coach:	So where would this be happening – this more support, more talking and more interest?
Worker:	Well pretty well everywhere – but mostly in the office where it is most obvious.
Manager–coach:	OK, so what would the rest of the team be noticing different about you?
Worker:	Oh, they'd see me initiating conversations with Rob.
Manager–coach:	And do you think that Rob would be pleased if you were initiating conversations?
Worker:	Yes I imagine.
Manager–coach:	So how might he respond – showing that he was pleased?
Worker:	The same way I suppose . . .

As soon as the team member is beginning the process of describing a possible better future rather than repetitiously recounting the story of the past there are already more possibilities for change and the manager–coach will now invite more interactive detail in the picture by tracking each difference and different response and each consequence of these, back and forth, interspersing the talking with repeated invitations to evaluate:

- 'Would you be pleased to see him doing that?'
- 'How might you respond if you were pleased to see him being more friendly?'
- 'Would he be pleased to see you taking an interest in his work again?'
- 'How would that be good for you if the two of you began to work more closely together again?'
- 'If the office were to be a more relaxed place to be in what way would that be good for you?'

Only after the picture of change has been developed in detail will the manager–coach move to separate the *ends* from the posited *means* 'OK – this is going to be really hard for you to imagine – imagine that the changes that you have described begin to happen even though no one has apologised – what do you think that you might notice different that will indicate to you that change has started even though the apology never came?' Once the worker can begin to imagine that, change divorced from apology, the likelihood of change is hugely increased. Somewhat paradoxically the likelihood of change is increased the more that the manager–coach can resist the inevitable pressure to indicate to the worker that the worker should be doing something different to resolve the situation. The challenge for the coach is to stay in the language of curiosity rather than to shift over into the rhetoric of persuasion. As soon as the team member begins to feel that the manager–coach is instructing her to do something different, then the 'not-my-fault' narrative is more likely to re-emerge and the worker retreats into the rigidity of 'it's his fault and he needs to take the first step'. 'Banging people's heads together' however tempting, is rarely the most effective step, particularly if the conflict has become entrenched.

Another route towards possibility lies through inviting the aggrieved team member to describe how she would know that the other party to the conflict genuinely wanted things to be better between them whether or not a formal apology was given. 'I guess saying sorry might mean something and might mean nothing – what would you see him doing that told you that he genuinely wants things to be different, that he is walking the walk and not just talking the talk?' Developing this description will serve to increase the chances that the aggrieved team member will begin to notice that the other party to the conflict is already doing things, however small, that fit with the description of someone who wants change to happen, and just noticing this is likely to make a reciprocal response more possible.

Scaling the commitment to make things better through the eyes of the other can also provide a pathway into flexibility.

Manager–coach:	On a scale of zero to ten with ten standing for your total commitment to making things better between the two of you and zero standing for the opposite where would Rob see you on that scale?
Worker:	Oh he'd probably say just about zero really. He thinks that I'm not prepared to be flexible at all – but that's just not right – I do want things to move forward.
Manager–coach:	OK so imagine that when Rob comes in tomorrow he sees something in you that lets him see how much you do really want things to move on, what are the smallest things that he would notice about you that would show him how much you want things to move forward?
Worker:	Probably if I were to ask him something.
Manager–coach:	Like what?
Worker:	Oh probably something about budget allocation – he's always been good on that and it's never really been my area.
Manager–coach:	If you were to ask him a question – maybe about budget allocation that would be a sign – what else might he notice about you that would show him evidence of your commitment to moving things forward?

In situations like this, where very often the manager is more obviously committed to the change than the aggrieved worker, the main challenge for the manager is to trust the process – just to invite the worker into a description and to trust the process to facilitate the change rather than attempting to pin down the changes by a time-lined commitment to specific differences.

High-performance meetings

Another area where solution focus can prove its worth to the manager is in the fine-tuning of meeting processes. Given the amount of time and energy that are expended in meetings in most organisations it is maybe surprising that relatively little attention is paid to making meetings work, which in turn is maybe associated with the complaint often heard 'I spend all my time in meetings and find it impossible to get on with my work'. Meetings rather than being experienced by employees as energising are often experienced as the exact opposite, stultifying in a way that reduces the level of engagement with the organisation and its goals. Michael Harker (2001), in a chapter entitled 'How to build solutions at meetings', seeks to partially explain this phenomenon by focusing on the problem domination that is characteristic of most meetings. For any organisation searching for a competitive edge in their sector having the most effective meetings of all their competitors would probably ensure above average performance. Those meetings that are experienced as productive, exciting, enjoyable and a good use of the resource that is poured into them are rare indeed.

Constructive openings

Nancy Kline wrote in *Time to Think* (1999: 107) 'People think better throughout the meeting if the very first thing they do is to say something true and positive about their work or how the work of the group is going'. This offers a simple way of building a resourceful context at the beginning of a meeting, simply inviting each of the meeting members to start by describing something that they have done at work since the last time the group met that has 'pleased you' or 'made you proud'. The more times this question can be circulated round the group, within the constraints of the time available, the more likely that it is to make a difference. The question can be alternated with asking 'so what have each of us seen in another team member's work since the last time we met that has made us proud to be a member of this team'. This very straightforwardly gives each meeting member an opportunity to compliment a colleague on a piece of work that otherwise might have risked going unnoticed and uncomplimented. Interestingly one of the Gallup Q12 questions, developed by the Gallup Organisation and stated by them to be one of the most significant questions in distinguishing between higher and lower performing work groups, is the question 'In the last seven days have I received recognition or praise for good work?' (Buckingham and Coffman, 1999: 28)

Starting each meeting with a brief review of what is working can have a huge impact on the subsequent quality of the meeting but it is not easy to do. For one thing it is counter-cultural to the informal processes in an organisation, it runs counter to the idea that we should not blow our own trumpets, it can be misread as 'Pollyanna'-ism and as taking up valuable time. Basically it takes nerve and to do it without confidence, or at least without the appearance of confidence, is to risk failure. The brave, however, will find that it works and will keep on doing it with an occasional variation:

- 'What have you done that you are pleased about?'
- 'What have you done that reminds you of why you wanted this job?'
- 'What have you valued in your colleagues?'
- And even a shift into the future: 'If you were at your best during this meeting how would the rest of us know?'

Purpose: An outcome focus

It is very easy to confuse purpose with purposefulness. A chairperson might begin by saying: 'The purpose of this meeting is to discover what went wrong'.

Although this sounds like a purposeful statement it is one that is likely to lead the meeting into an unproductive discussion since there are likely to be a number of equally plausible answers each backed by a barrage of facts and even more interpretations. A more trusting chairperson would ask: 'What are your best hopes from this meeting?'

This trust would not be without foundation but based on experience that if everyone is engaged in this negotiation everyone is more likely to contribute constructively even when their own views are not as accepted as they would like.

Chairperson: What are your best hopes from this meeting?

1st member: We need to find out exactly what went wrong.

Chairperson: And if we did that what difference do you hope it would make?

1st member: Then at least we'd know what not to do in future!

Chairperson: And?

1st member: We could start to think about what we could do instead.

Chairperson: So if we finished this meeting with some ideas about what we might do next that will have made it a productive meeting from your point of view?

1st member: Absolutely.

2nd member: I agree we need to move on but it's important we learn from this so we do need to find out exactly what happened.

3rd member: I'm not so sure. We could spend the whole meeting going round in circles. I think we should move on.

It is easy to see how within a few minutes everyone will be committed to a meeting that produces ideas about the future – a purposeful, outcome-oriented meeting. There will be differences about the process – how the meeting moves towards this outcome but the overall purpose will be shared. In these circumstances the chairperson might decide simply to divide the time: so much for inquest, so much for future planning. A solution focused chairperson might make a more creative use of this division.

Chairperson:	Let's get on with it! I propose we begin by looking forward and then review what we've learned already to see how that might help us move forward. So let's begin with a bit of 'blue sky': if we were to move forward in the way we each hope what would we start to notice different about the place?
1st member:	I'd think there would be a few brighter faces around for a start!
Chairperson:	So what would be making your face brighter?
1st member:	The first thing would be more cooperation between departments, especially marketing and production.
Chairperson:	How would you know that was happening?
1st member:	Because there wouldn't be so many foul-ups!
Chairperson:	*(Quietening the erupting argument with the next question)* So what would you be seeing happening between the two groups that led you to think more cooperation was happening?
1st member:	For one thing you'd see them talking.

This degree of focus, on the future rather than the past, permits little space for energy-wasting arguments and if the questions are carefully enough placed it is not long before potential strategies begin to emerge. Most importantly, they will emerge not so much as an answer to a complaint but as part of a shared view about a way forward. The head of production might try to blame foul-ups on the head of sales but both are likely to agree that cooperation makes sense and if they haven't had a chance to develop their animosity there will be more chance of cooperation.

When enough time has been spent on the future the solution focused chairperson will then put a creative spin on the past.

Chairperson:	So now let's look at how far we have come. What is already in place? What foundation have we already got to build this future on?
2nd member:	We have to learn from our mistakes.

Chairperson: Absolutely! We don't want to throw the baby out with the bath water! So what did we do right even though we made mistakes as well?

3rd member: Well, you couldn't argue with the fact that everyone put their backs into it; there was a lot of hard work and commitment.

Chairperson: What else? What else is there to build on?

Instead of looking at past problems the team looks at past successes addressing the problem areas through what was positively rather than negatively learned. This process will usually add to potential strategies for the future, one obvious one being to appreciate staff for their hard work rather than depress them with hints of blame for the failure.

Summary

Where the interests of the worker and those of the organisation coincide the manager–coach will be able to use the solution focused coaching process unchanged. This will be the case with most of the staff development issues that the manager is likely to face.

Unlike the disinterested coach the manager–coach will have an interest in the satisfactory performance of their worker and in certain circumstances will therefore be obliged to place issues on the coaching agenda and to invite the worker–client's engagement in the change process through a specification of what the implications of no change on the part of the worker are likely to be. When 'buy-in' is achieved the work can be treated as if the contract emanates from the client, although of course the manager–coach will also need to monitor progress, checking performance in a way that would not be necessary for the disinterested coach.

- Solution focus can be simply and straightforwardly used to manage and to resolve conflicts, between team members, between sections and between departments.
- Solution focus offers the manager useful tools for increasing the effectiveness of meetings; to create a context of creativity and to energise participants.

- Solution focus also facilitates the manager in reviewing and fine-tuning meeting processes, offering appreciative methods for helping participants to take responsibility for their own performance and contribution towards good outcomes.

Activities

Activity 1: Indirect influence

This activity can be undertaken in pairs with one acting as coach or it can be done alone with writing materials. The key to its effectiveness in generating change is in the detail. Descriptions need to be specific and concrete and as far as possible located at particular times in particular places.

- Bring to mind a member of staff with whom you are having difficulties.
- Describe (to your coach or on paper) ten specific and observable changes you would like this person to make in order to do the job they need to do in a way that supports the needs of colleagues and the aims of the organisation.
- Imagine that this person actually makes all of these changes (if you think this is impossible imagine a miracle has occurred); now list ten specific and observable changes in the way you would respond to this person whose behaviour has changed for the better.
- Over the next week look out for spontaneous improvements.

This activity would be one of the starting points for taking issue with a poorly performing colleague. Even if it does not lead to improvements it will shed a clearer light on the problem and help provide a focus for a more direct approach.

Activity 2: Making meetings work

This is an activity that can be done alone but which is particularly effective when performed by a whole team each member with his or her own scale and lists. The combined lists then provide both a strong foundation on which to build and significant pointers to better practice.

- Recall the last meeting that you attended.
- On a scale with ten representing the meeting could not have been more effective and zero representing the opposite where would you scale that meeting?
- Ten things (at least) that put the meeting there and not lower.
- Four things (the smaller the better) that you would be noticing at the next meeting if it was to score one point more on your scale.

11

Last words

Anyone waiting for a high impact punchline, a final key to make sense of the solution focused approach will be disappointed. A truly solution focused conversation should be hardly more than a whisper and for the highest impact of all it should not even hint at future action but remain solely in the realm of description: what might be and what already is.

BRIEF's is not the only solution focused model but it is the gentlest and briefest and manages this while being as effective as longer, more obviously interventive, versions. In response to a case presented to an email supervision group several solution focused approaches were offered. The client, Xavier, had lost all confidence and couldn't see how he could possibly attend a series of forthcoming interviews beginning in 3 weeks. Many suggestions worked from the starting point that attending the first interview was the goal and the purpose of the coaching was to help make this happen. Interest was expressed in how Xavier had managed successful interviews in the past, scaling his confidence that he would attend the interview and what he would need to do to move one point up the scale. Another strand was that the 3-week deadline was close and possibly pressurising. This seemed to be a deeper, longer-lasting problem that might require a longer-term approach even if this round of interviews had to be missed. The aim then would be to work on confidence building rather than solving the specific problem of attendance at the interviews. This appears to make sense until the most cursory look at research shows little correlation between the presented issue and the number of sessions needed to resolve it. What is most likely to lead to long term work is the coach's belief that long-term work will be necessary. Here lies another of the disciplines of solution focused practice: assumptions need constant testing. It is a safe assumption that a long-standing, life-governing, serious and complex problem is going to take time to resolve; it didn't develop overnight and it is not going to disappear overnight. Except when you look at research and find that this obvious 'truth' does not hold water. In fact, it is more likely to be resolved in one session than any other number of sessions.

BRIEF's approach would have been to see the return of Xavier's confidence as the contract and to trust that he would then make the best decision about the interviews when the time for them came round. The interviews would not in themselves be a target for the work. Most commonly the client would be invited to imagine waking up tomorrow with all his confidence back and build up a description of what differences this would make to the day. The key would be in the detail. If Xavier can describe in concrete tangible detail what difference having his confidence back (including the confidence to attend interviews) will make he is likely to begin 'doing' his life in that way. As he begins to 'live' confidence he is likely also to feel it and attending interviews would just be a small part of a much more encompassing preferred future.

It is this 'walking alongside' position that characterises BRIEF's current work. It leaves everything to the client so that any progress made can only be the client's own work. BRIEF's outcome studies do not show this to be any more (or less) effective than other variations but it has coincided with a significant drop in the average number of sessions, currently 2.25, attended by clients. BRIEF's understanding of this dramatic response to such a gentle touch is little more than homespun: if you discover an easier, more satisfying way of getting on with the day (and the next, and the next . . .) why wouldn't you do it? Imagine that you drive to work each day. You've found the best route and have used it for months or even years. Your car needs some repairs and a colleague offers to pick you up the next morning. You are grateful but also somewhat alarmed when she turns left at the lights where you normally go straight on. You say this but your colleague drives on confidently. The route is more scenic and is 10 minutes shorter. The next day, back in your own car what do you do at the traffic lights? A week or so later you are preoccupied and your automatic pilot takes you straight on at the lights. Do you resign yourself to going the long way for the rest of your life or do you remind yourself to pay more attention tomorrow?

One of the dangers of psychological theory in its ever growing complexity is that it can hide the obvious from us. In real life we are adjusting our routes every day as we deal with the mainly small and sometimes large obstacles and diversions that litter the way. Mostly, we do not even notice what we are doing and when we do notice it is usually because we have taken the wrong route, and the way through turned out to be a cul-de-sac. Perhaps all that solution focused coaching does is remind us of our manoeuvring skills when we think we are stuck. Once reminded we then get on with finding the right way forward. And it is 'finding a way forward', 'getting back on track' which are two of the most common contracts in solution focused coaching. As we have seen the solution focused approach is founded on a series of questions, and the task and skill of the solution focused coach is to construct a sequence of questions that are on the one hand fitting – fitting well enough with the client's world situation to make sense to him – and at the same time move the conversation in the direction of possibilities. The additional challenge is to do this in a way that indicates to the client that he is being listened to and this is best done by asking questions that take account of the client's last answer. If the question asked makes no sense in relation to what the client has just said then it would be reasonable for the client to assume that the coach is not listening whereas if the opposite is the case then the client's experience is likely to be favourable.

So, the solution focused coach will need to be flexible, will be constantly shaping the questions that he is asking in relation to focus, wording and tone and at the same time will be keeping in mind an overall map of the process, charting where on that map the conversation is in order to remain oriented even when sensitivity to the client demands a detour. As this map becomes more familiar the coach becomes more able to listen and so concentrate on what the client is saying rather than struggling to find a way among a mass of competing possible directions. Something else that makes the process easier is when the solution focused coach begins to realise that there are a number of questions that fit together into sequences and that those sequences, when the time is right, can be followed without the coach needing to question or necessarily to consider each step through the sequence. If the first question fits, very often the whole of the sequence will make sense.

An example of a useful sequence is a scale question. Having decided what the top and the bottom of the scale are to be, the coach will not need to consider each of the subsequent questions since 'where are you now?' can normally be followed by 'and what tells you that things are there and not lower?' which in turn can be followed by a series of 'what else?' questions which in turn can be followed by a series of 'one point up on the scale' questions often with some other person perspective questions to help to fill in the detail. This sequence makes sense and is usually very productive for the client. The coach simply needs to trust the process and listen carefully to each answer so the expression of the next question has a good fit, for example, in a 'what else?' series the coach might choose to amplify a particular answer before going on to the next what else? For example, 'That sounds hard, how did you manage to do that?'

Other examples of these sequences can be found when the client is asked to imagine a tomorrow in which his hopes have been realised. Following this initial proposition the coach will not have to think too hard when asking 'how will you know?' followed by a series of 'how else?'s' and then asking a series of other person perspective questions about who will notice first and what they will see, followed by an invitation to the client to think about what the first signs of the preferred future happening might be. Once the solution focused coach is familiar with a series of these sequences, then they can be put together into entire solution focused conversations and less decision making is required at each and every point in the conversation, leaving the coach to focus on fitting with the client.

A straightforward two-part conversation that the solution focused coach will use repeatedly is merely constructed from a preferred future sequence and then a scale. At any point that the client expresses an aspiration in a meeting, the coach is likely to respond by asking the client to describe the difference that the achievement of that aspiration would make. A series of 'how would you know?' questions can be interspersed with some 'what difference would that make?' questions and in order to fill out the detail a number of other person perspective questions concentrating on 'who would notice?' and 'what would they see?' Having invited the client to paint the picture of the achievement of their aspiration in concrete real-life terms the coach can simply ask a scale question. This will allow the client to determine how much of the aspired to state is already in place and how he will know that things have moved one point nearer to ten.

Solution focused coaching is a simple business. Even children can be taught to do it – just as children can be taught a new language. And that is a good way to see learning solution focused coaching. It is simple but not easy and like any new language it only comes with practice. This book has laid out the grammar, given sample conversations and set homework. Anyone with enough friends and family or even intrepid clients to practise on could teach themselves how to be a solution focused coach from this book. It was how BRIEF started: teaching ourselves from de Shazer's *Clues*. So we know it is possible.

Appendix

Solution focused questions

Problem-free talk

'I know very little about you apart from a little about what brings you here.'

'What would you feel happy to tell me about yourself?'

'What are you interested in?'

'What do you enjoy?'

'What are you good at?'

'What about family?'

'How would your best friend describe you?'

Pre-treatment change

'Often between making an appointment and arriving for that appointment people have already noticed a change. What changes have you noticed?' or 'Have you noticed a change?'

Establishing a common contract

'What are your best hopes from our talking together?'

'How will you know that our talking together has been useful to you?'

'What will it take for you to say that this has been worthwhile?'

Preferred future

'Imagine that you wake up tomorrow and (your best hopes are all happening). How will you know? What will be different?'

'Imagine that after you have gone to bed tonight, a miracle happens and (your best hopes are all happening). But since you are asleep, you will not know that the miracle has happened. When you wake up tomorrow morning what will be different that will tell you? What will you see yourself doing differently, what will you see others doing differently that will tell you that the miracle has happened?'

'What will be the first sign of the miracle happening?'

'What small step would be a sign of moving in the right direction/being on the right track?'

'How will you know that life is going well for you?'

'What will tell you that you don't need to come here any more?'

'Imagine a day going well for you. How will you know that the day is going well?'

'And if this problem were resolved, what would be different in your life that would tell you?'

'How will you know that you are living a life that does you justice?'

'How will you know that you are performing (at work) in a way that does your skills, strengths, talents and competencies full justice?'

Instances

'So tell me about the times that you are more confident?'

'So when was the last time that you did manage to speak up for yourself in a way that was good for you and good for the team?'

'When are the times that you notice a little of the resilience that you would like to see more of at work?'

Exceptions

'When are the times that it doesn't happen?'

'When are the times that it doesn't last as long?'

'When are the times that it seems to be less intense?'

'When are the times that it bothers you least?'

'When do you resist the urge to . . . ?'

'What are you doing differently and what are others doing that is different at those (exception) times?'

Coping

'So what has been helping you to survive?'

'How have you been getting through?'

'How come you have not given up hope?'

'So how come you have managed to get here today?'

'What do you think your (best friend) most admires about the way that you have been struggling with this?'

'How do you cope?'

'That situation sounds pretty overwhelming; how do you get by?'

'What do you do that helps you to get through?'

'What is it that gives you the strength to even get up in the morning?'

Stopping things getting worse

'So what have you been doing to stop things getting even worse?'

'So how come you aren't at (minus three) on your scale?'

'You say that things have gone down on the scale. What did you do to stop the slide at four?'

Scales

'On a scale of zero to ten, with zero being the worst that things have been and ten representing how you want things to be, where are you today?'

'So what is it that you are doing that means that you are at . . . and not at zero?'

'So if you are on three, tell me what you will be doing that will tell you that you are on four?'

'Where on that scale represents good enough for you, the point that you would settle for? How will you know that you are there?'

'On a scale of zero to ten where would you rate your desire for change?'

'What would be happening when it is one point higher?'

'On a similar scale how do you rate your confidence that the problem will be resolved?'

'When your relationship with your (boss) moves up one point what difference do you think this will make to you at work generally?'

'On a scale of zero to ten how confident do you feel of keeping (yourself) safe?'

Locating resources, building on strengths

'When you faced this sort of problem in the past how did you resolve it?'

'How would you know that you were doing that again?'

'What other tough situations have you handled?'

'What did handling that well tell you about yourself?'

'What is your approach to finding solutions to tough situations?'

View of self

'What does this (achievement) teach you about yourself?'

'What do you now know about yourself that you didn't know last week?'

'Was that a surprise to you?'

'What have you learned from this experience?'

'What have you learned from this experience that will be useful to you in your future?'

Follow-up sessions

'What's been better?'

'What's different?'

'What have you been pleased with?'

'What's been telling you that life is moving in a good direction for you?'

'Tell me about the times that you were at (scale point + 1) since we last met?'

Constructive history

'Who would be least surprised by this change that you have made, this achievement?'

'What did that person know about you that others did not know?'

'When in the past have you seen yourself drawing usefully on the self-same qualities that you drew on to make this change?'

'What in the past have you achieved that is in some way similar to this?'

'Looking back what tells you that you always were capable of doing this?'

'When else, in the past, have you noticed yourself drawing on similar qualities?'

'Have you always been a survivor or did you have to learn the hard way?'

'It sounds like you needed to look after yourself from a very early age – when did you first realise you had the capacity to do this?'

'How do you manage to keep your sense of humour – is this one of the qualities you have which has kept you going?'

Other person perspective

'How will (your colleague) know that the miracle has happened?'

'Who will be the first person to notice that things have moved up one point on your scale?'

'Who will be the hardest to convince that you mean business this time and what will she need to see?'

'What will HR need to see you doing to feel more confident that you have a future with this organisation?'

What else?

'What else?' 'What else?' 'What else?' 'What else?' 'What else?' 'What else?' 'What else?' 'What else?' 'What else?' 'What else?'

Footnote on questions

Questions lie at the heart of solution focused brief therapy. In the solution focused approach the coach does not 'tell' clients, she asks questions that allows the client to 'tell' herself and in so doing to reconstruct her world in a way that can make a difference.

In asking questions the coach is not seeking to gain information about the content of the client's answer and thus to become more and more expert on the client and the client's world. Rather the questions are a provocation to the client to think differently.

And of course, as de Shazer makes clear, you cannot know what question you have asked until the client answers it!

References

Berg, I. K. and Miller, S. (1992) *Working with the Problem Drinker: A Solution Focused Approach.* New York: Norton.

Berg, I. K. and Szabo, P. (2005) *Brief Coaching for Lasting Solutions.* New York: Norton.

Binney, G. and Williams, C. (1995) *Leaning into the Future.* London: Nicholas Brealey.

Buckingham, M. and Coffman, C. (1999) *First, Break all the Rules.* Gallup Organisation.

Cade, B. (2009) Monty Python-focused therapy. In E. Connie and L. Metcalf (Eds.), *The Art of Solution-Focused Therapy.* New York: Springer Publishing Company.

Cooperrider, D. and Whitney, D. (1999) *Appreciative Inquiry.* San Francisco, CA: Berrett-Koehler.

de Shazer, S. (1983) *Patterns of Brief Family Therapy.* New York: Guilford Press.

de Shazer, S. (1984) The death of resistance. *Family Process, 23*: 11–17.

de Shazer, S. (1985) *Keys to Solution in Brief Therapy.* New York: Norton.

de Shazer, S. (1987) Minimal elegance. *Networker, Sept–Oct*: 57–60.

de Shazer, S. (1988) *Clues: Investigating Solutions in Brief Therapy.* New York: Norton.

de Shazer, S. (1991) *Putting Difference to Work.* New York: Norton.

de Shazer, S., Berg, I. K., Lipchik, E., Nunnally, E., Molnar, A., Gingerich, W. and Weiner-Davis, M. (1986) Brief therapy: focused solution development. *Family Process, 25*: 207–221.

Dolan, Y. (1991) *Resolving Sexual Abuse.* New York: Norton.

Flaherty, J. (1999) *Coaching: Evoking Excellence in Others.* Boston: Butterworth-Heinemann.

Flückiger, C. and Grosse Holtforth, M. (2008) Focusing the therapist's attention on the patient's strengths: A preliminary study to foster a mechanism of change in outpatient psychotherapy. *Journal of Clinical Psychology, 64*(7): 876–890.

Gassman, D. and Grawe, K. (2006) General change mechanisms: The relation between problem activation and resource activation in successful and unsuccessful therapeutic interactions. *Clinical Psychology and Psychotherapy, 13*: 1–11.

George, E., Iveson, C. and Ratner, H. (1999) *Problem to Solution: Brief Therapy with Individuals and Families* (2nd ed.). London: BT Press.

Greene, J. and Grant, A. (2003) *Solution -Focused Coaching.* Harlow: Pearson.

Harker, M. (2001) How to build solutions at meetings In Y. Ajmal and I. Rees (Eds.), *Solutions in Schools: Creative Applications of Solution Focused Brief Thinking with Young People and Adults.* London: BT Press.

Jackson, P. Z. (2006) *Improvisation skills for trainers and coaches.* Conference presentation at SF Trainers' Conference, Amsterdam.

Jackson, P. Z. and McKergow, M. (2002) *The Solutions Focus.* London: Nicholas Brealey.

Kahane, A. (2004) *Solving Tough Problems.* San Francisco, CA: Berrett-Koehler.

Kline, N. (1999) *Time to Think.* London: Ward Lock.

Korman, H. (2004) *The Common Project.* Malmo, Sweden: Sikt. Retrieved *www.sikt.nu* on 25 July 2011.

Lee, M. Y., Sebold, J. and Uken, A. (2003) *Solution-Focused Treatment of Domestic Violence Offenders: Accountability for Change.* Oxford: Oxford University Press.

Lipchik, E. (1988) Interviewing with a Constructive Ear. *Dulwich Centre Newsletter, Winter*, 3–7.

Lipchik, E. and de Shazer, S. (1986). The purposeful interview. *Journal of Strategic and Systemic Therapies, 5*(1&2): 88–99.

McFarland, B. (1995) *Brief Therapy and Eating Disorders.* San Francisco: Jossey-Bass.

Miller, G. and de Shazer, S. (1998) Have you heard the latest rumor about . . .? Solution-focused therapy as a rumor. *Family Process, 37*: 363–377.

Nicholas, L. (2008) *Introduction to Psychology* (2nd ed.). Cape Town: UCT Press.

Nylund, D. and Corsiglia, V. (1994) Becoming solution-focused forced in brief therapy: Remembering something important we already knew. *Journal of Systemic Therapies, 13*(1): 5–12.

O'Connell, B. (2001) *Solution Focused Stress Counselling.* London: Continuum.

O'Hanlon, B. (2001) *The Art of Therapeutic Problem Solving.* Two-day presentation – BRIEF, London.

O'Hanlon, B. and Martin, M. (1992) *Solution-Oriented Hypnosis.* New York: Norton.

Peltier, B. (2009) *The Psychology of Executive Coaching: Theory and Application.* London: Routledge.

Pemberton, C. (2006) *Coaching to Solutions.* Oxford: Butterworth-Heinemann.

Secretan, L. (2004) *Inspire! What Great Leaders Do.* Hoboken: Wiley.

Starr, J. (2003). *The Coaching Manual.* London: Prentice Hall.

Wade, A. (1997) Small acts of living: Everyday resistance to violence and other forms of oppression. *Contemporary Family Therapy,* *19*(1): 23–39.

Weiner-Davis, M., de Shazer, S. and Gingerich, W. (1987) Constructing the therapeutic solution by building on pretreatment change: An exploratory study. *Journal of Family and Marital Therapy,* *13*(4): 359–363.

White, M. (2001) *Narrative Therapy.* Two-day presentation – BRIEF, London.

Whitmore, J. (1996) *Coaching for Performance* (2nd ed.). London: Nicholas Brealey.

Index